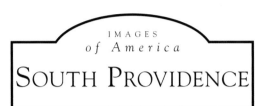

IMAGES
of America

SOUTH PROVIDENCE

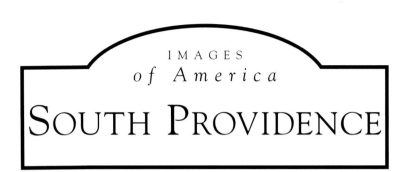

IMAGES
of America

SOUTH PROVIDENCE

Patrick T. Conley and Paul Campbell

ARCADIA
PUBLISHING

Published by Arcadia Publishing
Charleston SC, Chicago IL, Portsmouth NH, San Francisco CA

Printed in the United States of America

Library of Congress Catalog Card Number: 2006923200

For all general information contact Arcadia Publishing at:
Telephone 843-853-2070
Fax 843-853-0044
E-mail sales@arcadiapublishing.com
For customer service and orders:
Toll-Free 1-888-313-2665

Visit us on the Internet at www.arcadiapublishing.com

*Dedicated to Mary Beatrice Conley (Aunt Mary)
and Irene and Roland Campbell (Mom and Dad)*

CONTENTS

ACKNOWLEDGMENTS

Many minds and many hands contribute to the making of a book—and this one was no exception. Our debt is large. Photographer Peter Goldberg took pictures of those existing buildings that shaped our story and reproduced many images for our use. John Myers, the knowledgeable and gracious Providence city archivist, assisted in the research and verification of a multitude of dates and addresses. Colleen Conley helped us to collect photographs and data; Linda Gallen and Anna Loiselle typed the manuscript; and 98-year-old Julia V. Conley (née Maney) shared her neighborhood reminiscences with us. George Pearson, a retired Providence police officer, Jeffrey Emidy of the State Historical Preservation and Heritage Commission, and Anne Sherman and George Goodwin of the Rhode Island Jewish Historical Association were helpful above and beyond our expectations. A score of individuals and organizations responded to our request for images and memorabilia. They are mentioned specifically in our captions. We hope this book is worthy of their efforts.

Like most photo albums, this one is both episodic and subjective. The scarcity of photographs, space limitations, the emphasis of the series on bygone generations rather than contemporary developments, and the need to balance scholarship with sentimentality have combined to make our pictorial history more nostalgic than up-to-date and analytical. Nonetheless, we believe that it captures the spirit of old South Providence, and, like an image, stirs both the imagination and the memory.

—Patrick T. Conley and Paul R. Campbell

INTRODUCTION

South Providence is a local geographic area, a city neighborhood, and a state of mind. Its historic boundaries, at least since 1868, when most of it was reannexed by Providence from Cranston, can be delineated with considerable (although not perfect) precision.

The boundaries we have selected begin on Point Street at the bridge over the Providence River, run due west to Plain Street, then to Beacon Avenue, and follow the latter two blocks northwest to Broad Street where the YMCA building is located. The boundary then runs along Broad Street (the old Pequot Trail) a distance of exactly two miles to the Harbor Junction railroad spur, turns east along the railroad tracks to the river, and finally north along the waterfront to the Point Street Bridge. We have not included the Jewelry District adjacent to downtown, except for Point Street, nor the city's high school educational complex in the Hoyle Square area between Broad and Westminster Streets. These two sections have recently been added to South Providence by census statisticians, but neither was historically part of the Southside neighborhood.

The major north-south thoroughfares traversing South Providence are Allens Avenue along the river, Eddy Street, Plain Street, Ocean Street, Prairie Avenue, and Broad Street. The major east-west streets are Point, Pine, Friendship, Dudley, and Public Streets and Potters and Thurbers Avenues. Every major avenue contains a diverse mixture of residential, commercial, industrial, and institutional uses, except Allens Avenue, which became exclusively industrial after the acquisition of the waterfront by coal, gas, oil, electric, and chemical companies in the early 20th century.

City agencies now use Public Street to divide South Providence into "upper" (north) and "lower" for planning purposes, but we treat both as one. The Southside neighborhoods west of Broad Street (Elmwood and South Elmwood) and south of Harbor Junction (Washington Park) are not included in this pictorial reminiscence. They were also part of the 1868 reannexation from Cranston, a boundary change that was prompted in part by the desire of the Yankee Republican-controlled state legislature to blunt the rising political power of Irish Catholic Democrats.

Under the reapportionment scheme established by the state constitution of 1843, Providence was limited to one state senator and 12 representatives. By 1850, the city had reached the point where increases in the population had no impact on the size of its assembly delegation. Meanwhile, the working-class electors, many of them Irish, living just beyond the city limits were beginning to threaten Republican control of Cranston (and North Providence and Johnston as well).

To rescue themselves from Irish Democratic control, these Yankee Republican municipalities transferred their industrial areas to Providence, leaving the rural residue safety in the hands of the GOP. Through this process of political mitosis, Democratic Providence gained in area and population, while its legislative representation remained unchanged. In view of its origins, it was fitting that South Providence became a Democratic stronghold and a hotbed of political activity in the decades following its creation as a neighborhood of Providence. During the course of the 20th century, it produced three governors, a speaker of the House of Representatives, Rhode Island's longest-serving chief justice, the longest-serving presiding justice of the superior court, a chief judge of the family court, and a host of prominent legislators, jurists, and administrators.

The geographic and demographic developments of the 19th century provided the foundation for the economically diverse, blue-collar, densely populated, multicultural community of the 20th century. This community evolved from three principal areas of settlement that date from the middle decades of the 19th century: the Pine-Friendship Street corridor, Burgess Cove, and Dogtown. The latter two areas were part of the 1868 Cranston annexation.

The Pine-Friendship Street area, referred to as "Upper, Upper South Providence," was always within the bounds of Providence. In June 1781, the site served as the initial campgrounds for the French army as Count Rochambeau's troops, over 4,000 strong, began their fateful march to Yorktown. A half century later, its location, just west of the Jewelry District and within walking distance of downtown, made it attractive to middle- and upper-class Providence businessmen. In 1832, a subdivision of the Providence Aqueduct Company's large tract paved the way for residential development in this northern section of South Providence and marked the beginning of a neighborhood. Most of those merchants and entrepreneurs who moved to this area from the 1840s onward acquired homes built by contractor-builders like William Clark and William H. Dyer, both of whom resided in the neighborhood, or by speculators such as Gov. D. Russell Brown, who lived just beyond its borders.

By the late 19th century, the Pine-Friendship enclave was fully built with impressive Greek Revival, Italianate, Queen Anne, and Second Empire single-family homes, many of which could be described as mansions. Here resided old-stock Rhode Islanders, including Mayor William S. Hayward, textile magnate Benjamin B. Knight, jewelry manufacturers Stanton B. Champlin, John B. Wood, and Frederick I. Marcy, and the president of the Gorham Manufacturing Company, William H. Crins.

By the early 20th century, the expansion of mass transit encouraged affluent Pine Street residents to move to an outer ring of neighborhoods, such as Elmwood and Edgewood. As a result of such migration, ownership of their splendid homes passed to absentee landlords who converted many of them into apartment or rooming houses of varying quality and condition. The tenants were mainly poor adult whites. Some of the houses were put to commercial use (if prostitution can be considered such), and during World War II, Pine Street acquired a reputation as a red-light district. A vigorous historic preservation effort, begun in the 1970s, has restored most of the surviving structures to their original exterior splendor.

In 1832, the Rhode Island General Assembly issued a charter to the New York, Providence, and Boston Railroad Company to build a Providence-to-Westerly railroad. This grant was followed by a Connecticut charter allowing the extension of the proposed route to Stonington, providing a deepwater terminus and allowing passengers from Boston and Providence to board Long Island steamers bound for New York City. On November 10, 1837, the Providence-to-Stonington line was opened for traffic. Its rails approached Providence from the south along the present Harbor Junction spur to Burgess Cove. The track was soon extended northerly, paralleling the west bank of the Providence River, to a terminus on a wharf near the present hurricane barrier, from which passengers were ferried to the Boston and Providence depot at India Point.

The New York, Providence, and Boston Railroad spanned several coves via a causeway that later evolved into Allens Avenue, a riverfront thoroughfare named for speculator Benjamin J. Allen. The cove at Harbor Junction (the present terminus of Thurbers Avenue) drew its name from the Burgess family who farmed the area adjacent to its shoreline.

The railroad provided an impetus for development around Burgess Cove in the 1830s. The Pavilion Hotel, built to accommodate train travelers, stood on a hill overlooking the cove at the easterly end of Pavilion Avenue until it burned in 1857. This small settlement flourished until the early 1840s, when the railroad moved its terminus northward. A revival occurred in the early

1850s as working-class families built homes along the shore of the cove, while more prosperous businessmen and professionals occupied the high ground near present-day Eddy Street. Notable among the latter were lawyer Nathan Porter, a state representative from Cranston who actively promoted the development of the Burgess Cove community as a suburban neighborhood, and J. G. B. Fauvel Gaurand, the French vice-consul, who tried, persistently but unsuccessfully, to establish a steamship line between France and Providence.

Burgess Cove was filled from the 1890s onward, and its mixed-use neighborhood was gradually obliterated as Providence converted its outer harbor to heavy industrial use. Cove families (like the Conleys) moved west of Eddy Street and mingled with those families who moved southward from the notorious Irish immigrant settlement known as Dogtown.

The Dogtown community arose in the 1840s on the northern fringe of what was then Cranston between Willard Avenue and the town line at Dudley Street. Four slaughterhouses were built on Willard Avenue between Prairie Avenue and Broad Street, with stockyards extending north to Blackstone Street and the now-filled Oxen Pond. Dogs scavenged voraciously around the slaughterhouses, thereby giving the Irish settlement its pejorative name. On the Providence side of the old municipal boundary, the Rhode Island Bleachery (1838) at Eddy and Dudley Streets, the Providence Machine Company (1846), and the New England Screw Company (1852) provided jobs for the Irish immigrants who settled in and around Dogtown.

The main commercial artery of Dogtown was Prairie Avenue, where several stores and saloons were located, but the center of Irish community life was the Cathedral of SS. Peter and Paul, just north of the South Providence neighborhood, and St. Michael's, which began in 1857 as St. Bernard's mission chapel on Prairie Avenue at the corner of Oxford Street. Elevated to parish status in 1859 and dedicated to St. Michael in 1868 by pastor Michael Wallace, it was destined to become the most populous parish in the diocese and the socioreligious center of the predominantly Irish Catholic South Providence neighborhood. From the center of Blackstone Street northward, however, South Providence remained a part of the cathedral parish, which operated Bishop Tyler School on Point Street for the Catholic youth of the Pine-Friendship Street section.

The influence of Catholicism permeated South Providence, with the neighborhood's dominant religion symbolized by the massive Romanesque church of St. Michael the Archangel. When completed in 1915, nearly a quarter-century after its cornerstone was laid, it towered over a level landscape dotted mainly by three-decker tenements, small factories, and mom and pop stores and businesses.

For more than 90 years following the 1868 annexation, the Irish were South Providence's largest ethnic group, but from the 1890s through the 1950s, the neighborhood was also known for its sizable and significant Jewish population. This close-knit, vibrant, highly mercantile community, mainly from eastern Europe, was centered in the old Dogtown district near Willard and Prairie Avenues. The so-called Teutonic migration of the late 19th century added British Americans and Swedes to the mix—each with their own distinctive churches and social organizations.

In the early 20th century—specifically from 1913 to 1934—State Pier No. 1 on the South Providence waterfront welcomed immigrants from the Mediterranean, the Balkans, eastern Europe, and the Near East. These newcomers arrived on steamships of the Fabre Line, which was based in Marseilles, France. Of the approximately 84,000 immigrants who landed in South Providence, a small number ventured only a few hundred yards into their adopted land. Small pockets of Italians, Ukrainians, Russian Jews, Armenians, and Greeks thus became part of South Providence's ethnic stew, a mixture also flavored by French Canadians and Chinese in the area of Summer and Pine Streets.

In the two decades following World War II, the old ethnics fled from South Providence to the West Bay suburbs—especially Cranston and Warwick—or to more affluent city neighborhoods like Elmhurst and the East Side. This exodus was fueled by such diverse factors as the low-interest mortgages of the Federal Housing Administration, the upward mobility of the second and third generations, the obsolescence of the neighborhood's housing stock, the relocation of city businesses to the suburbs, the proliferation of the automobile, and the completion of Interstate 95 through South Providence and beyond.

In their wake, the departing ethnics left obsolete housing that was often reduced to vacant, litter-strewn lots. From the early 1960s onward, local blacks, dislocated from their traditional residential areas in Mount Hope, Lippitt Hill, Randall Square, and Benefit Street, moved to South Providence, where low rents and absentee landlords became the rule. The 744-unit Roger Williams Housing Project, completed in 1943, was transformed by 1970 into a black ghetto, where the locals were joined by African Americans from the South and from larger cities in the Northeast. Over a span of 30 years, black community leaders (most notably councilman Lloyd Griffin) and a host of neighborhood organizations like Stop Wasting Abandoned Property (SWAP) and Omni Development Corporation reversed the neighborhood decline and built hundreds of modern affordable-housing units. They also lobbied successfully for the establishment of an impressive and diverse array of educational facilities, capped by the Providence campus of the Community College of Rhode Island. In addition, Rhode Island Hospital and a relocated Women and Infants Hospital have overspread the old Dogtown settlement. Between 1966 and 1979, more than 61 percent of all residential units in Upper South Providence were demolished—a reduction in structures from 1,458 to 562.

In the past quarter-century (1980–2005), the neighborhood's tradition of diversity has been enhanced by the addition of a small Native American community; Africans from Liberia and Nigeria; Cambodians; Laotians; Hmong from the hills of Laos, who were dislocated by the Vietnam War; and Hispanics from a host of Caribbean and Central American countries, especially the Dominican Republic and Puerto Rico. During the 1990s, the Hispanic influx was so dramatic that the federal census of 2000 ranked Latinos as South Providence's largest ethno-cultural group, with over 50 percent of the total population, while African Americans accounted for 34 percent of the remaining neighborhood residents. Only time will reveal how another century of ethnic succession and economic development will alter the character of South Providence, but time will not change this pictorial record of our neighborhood's fascinating and poignant past.

One

THE YANKEES
UPPER, UPPER SOUTH
PROVIDENCE TO 1900

South Providence had its initial brush with history from June 11 through June 21, 1781, when it became the site of the first encampment of Count Rochambeau's army as America's French allies began their long march to Yorktown. This map of the camp, drawn by army cartographer Louis-Alexander Bertier, shows the French artillery emplacements on a rise of land near what would become Hayward Park. The shaded areas sloping toward the river depict the sites where the 4,000-man army bivouacked, while its officers stayed in the homes of prominent Providence residents. The "chemin de Pawtuxet" (upper right center) is Broad Street. Upon their departure, the troops took Cranston Street through Knightsville (then called Monkeytown) and made their second camp around Waterman's Tavern in Coventry, 15 miles distant from South Providence. (Courtesy of Howard C. Rice Jr. and Anne S. K. Brown.)

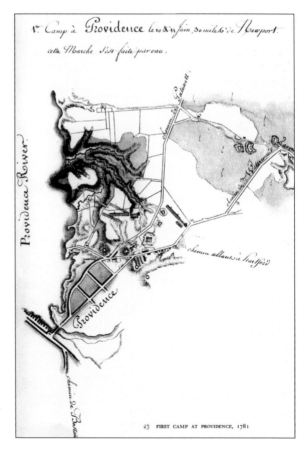

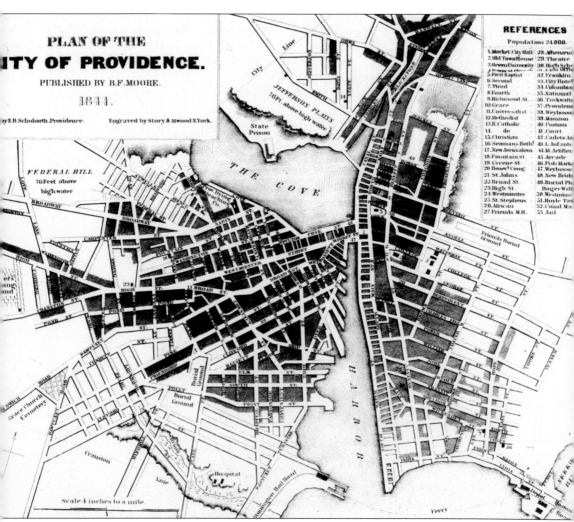

This 1844 map drawn by Nathanael Schubarth shows sparse development in the area that became part of the South Providence neighborhood. The Cranston line was located just south of the Marine Hospital (lower left center) along present-day Dudley Street. The West Burial Ground, the aqueduct tract, and the hospital lands posed obstacles to settlement. The authors have called this area—always within the Providence city limits—"Upper, Upper South Providence" because it was the most northerly and the most affluent portion of the neighborhood. (Courtesy of the authors.)

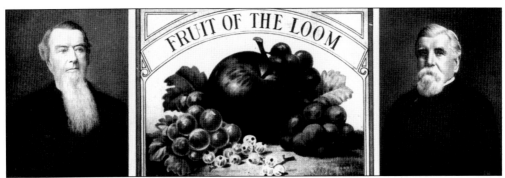

Benjamin R. (left) and Robert Knight formed what was reputedly the world's largest textile empire. The Knight brothers, sons of a Cranston farmer, began their illustrious careers as lowly operatives in the Sprague (now Cranston) Print Works, one of the many firms they came to own. In 1852, they formed their fateful partnership as co-owners of the Pontiac Mill in Warwick. By 1896, under their still famous trademark Fruit of the Loom, they owned 21 cotton mills with an aggregate capacity of 11,000 looms and over 400,000 spindles and employed nearly 7,000 operatives. Benjamin R. Knight (1813–1898) served the city as an alderman from South Providence and as a representative in the Rhode Island General Assembly. Robert Knight (1826–1912) was active in Providence banking circles. Both built splendid local residences—Benjamin on 159 Broad Street near Stewart Street (shown below), Robert on Elmwood Avenue. Both residences have since been demolished. Though their company went bankrupt in 1924, its famous label lives on. (Courtesy of the authors.)

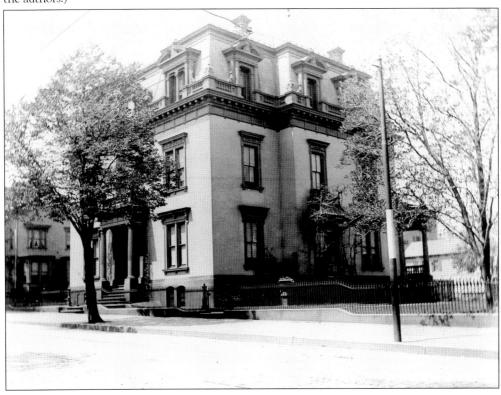

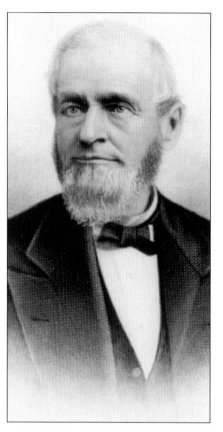

Amos Chafee Barstow (left) built a stove foundry on Point Street in 1849. Its Model Cook, shown below in an 1861 catalog, had a ventilated roasting oven, an innovation that earned it a national reputation. This company, which employed 200 workers and covered two and a half acres of the Point, Richmond, and Chestnut Streets block, won the Grand Medal of Merit at the 1873 Vienna World's Fair for the best cooking stoves and ranges. The company failed in 1930, and its main building is now occupied by the Tops Electric Supply Company. As remarkable as the corporate history of Barstow Stove is the career of its founder, Amos Chafee Barstow (1813–1892). In addition to his business pursuits, which included positions in banking, the litany of his achievements indicates his impact upon the history of his native city: mayor of Providence (1852–1853), Republican representative and House Speaker (1870), member of the Providence Common Council, trustee of the Dexter Donation, first president of the Providence YMCA, president of the Providence Association of Mechanics and Manufacturers, president of the board of Butler Hospital, and builder of the Providence Music Hall. He was also a published poet and essayist, a Congregational deacon, and a member and chairman of the U.S. Board of Indian Commissioners, to which he was appointed by Pres. Ulysses S. Grant. (Courtesy of the authors.)

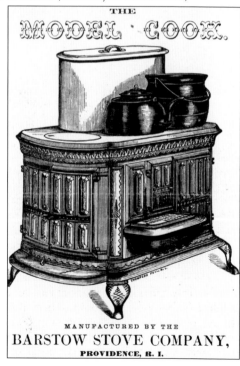

THE
MODEL · COOK.

MANUFACTURED BY THE
BARSTOW STOVE COMPANY,
PROVIDENCE, R. I.

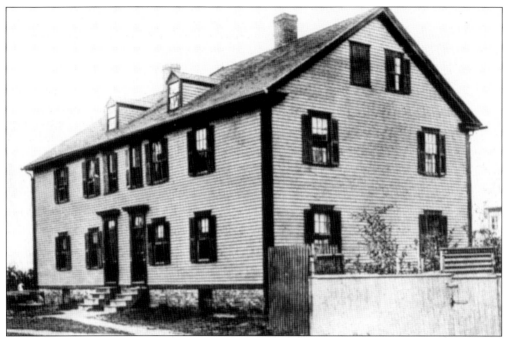

The Providence Yellow Fever Hospital was built in 1798 during a particularly severe yellow fever epidemic. It was originally located on a rise of land overlooking the river at what was then the extreme southeastern corner of Providence, on the present site of Rhode Island Hospital. When the epidemic had run its course, this facility was used to quarantine and care for sick and injured seamen and became known as the Marine Hospital. It was moved to Whately Street in 1863 to make room for the new hospital and was eventually demolished in 1963. (Courtesy of the authors.)

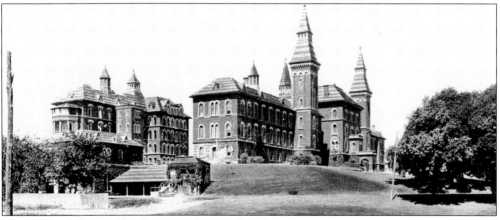

Rhode Island Hospital has been South Providence's most significant institution since it opened on October 1, 1868. Its site is near the old Providence-Cranston line on land originally occupied by the Marine Hospital. The movement for a modern health services facility had been led by Dr. Usher Parsons and the Providence Medical Association, but it took the generosity of the Ives family to provide the financial base for a successful public fund-raising effort. The original building (shown here in 1886) was demolished in 1956, and the lawn in the foreground is now the site of Hasbro Children's Hospital. Though dramatically different, Rhode Island Hospital continues to flourish and expand and is housed in several modern buildings. Today it is the state's largest private employer. (Courtesy of the authors.)

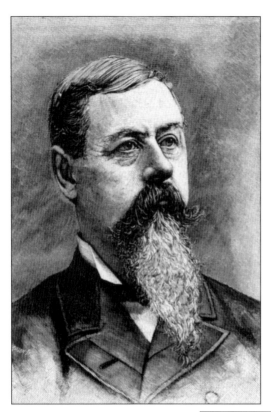

William S. Hayward was raised on a farm in Foster and came to Providence in 1851 at the age of 16. After gaining prominence as a manufacturer of bakery products, Hayward entered politics, serving as a member of the common council (1872–1876) and the board of alderman (1876–1880). In 1880, he was elected mayor of Providence and served with distinction in that capacity for three years before declining renomination. He lived at 432 Broad Street. (Courtesy of the authors.)

The fountain in Hayward Park, the oasis of Upper South Providence, was donated to the city in 1889 by Mayor Hayward. The two-acre park, once located between Plain Street and Beacon Avenue, was carved from the West Burial Ground. In the late 19th century, the park was considered as a possible location for the Rhode Island state capitol. It was obliterated in 1960 by the construction of Interstate 95. (Courtesy of the authors.)

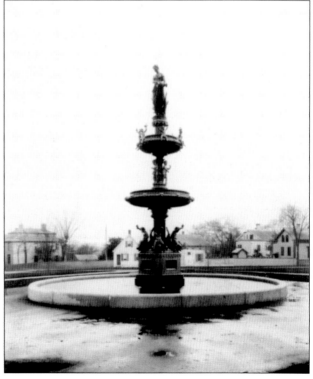

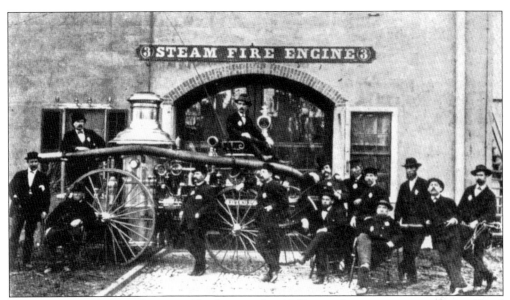

Fire King Steam Engine Company No. 3, created in 1860, was the successor to volunteer Hand Engine Company No. 5, whose motto, Mid the Raging Flames the Fire King Reigns, was adopted by the newly organized steam engine company shown here. Its station, built on Summer Street in 1840, remained Fire King's headquarters until 1875, when the company moved to a more modern facility on nearby Pond Street. In this 1860 photograph, the firefighters are posing with one of the first three steam fire engines purchased by the city, a rotary steamer built by the Silsby Company of Seneca Falls, New York. (Courtesy of the authors.)

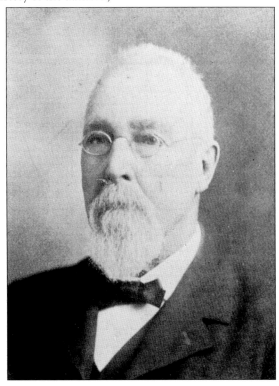

Oliver F. Greene, a resident of 49 Prairie Avenue, joined the Providence fire service in March 1854, following the establishment of the paid department. He worked as clerk for Fire King Hand Engine Company No. 5 for six years and then was assigned to Fire King Steam Engine Company No. 3 as its captain. Greene continued to move up the ranks, becoming second assistant engineer under Dexter Gorton in 1865. Four years later, he was elected chief engineer (fire chief). One biographical sketch written shortly after Greene's retirement cited the 30-year department veteran for being "a man of firm resolutions, a good organizer, and quite a disciplinarian." (Courtesy of the authors.)

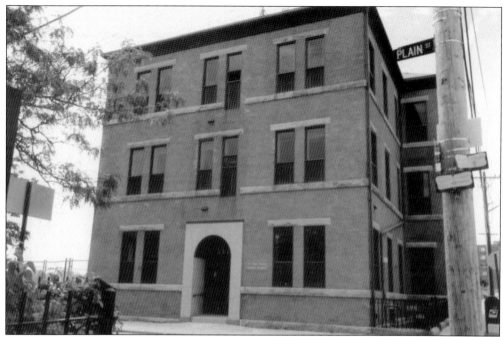

The 5th Precinct police headquarters was built on Plain Street in 1886, when the neighborhood became populous enough to require a police presence. The three-and-a-half-story brick and granite building housed the 5th Precinct until 1948, when the city converted it to the Plain Street Recreation Center. That use ended in 1970, and the structure eventually became a medical office building to serve nearby Rhode Island Hospital. (Courtesy of the authors.)

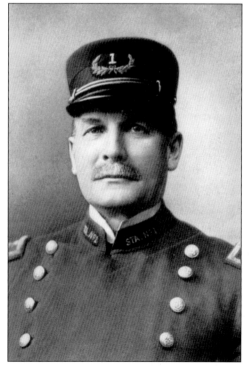

William H. Lawrence joined the police force in 1875. For several years, he had the Dogtown beat, and by 1894, he had risen to the number-two position at the 5th Precinct. After service elsewhere in the city, Lawrence returned once more to South Providence in 1906 as captain and commander of the district. (Courtesy of the Providence Police Department.)

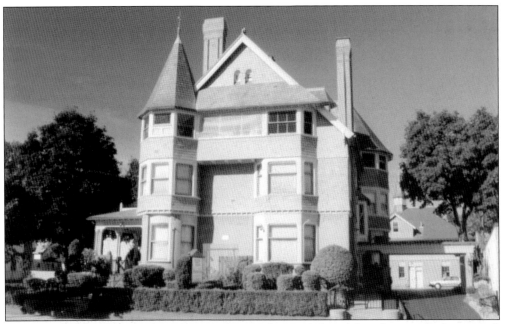

Upper South Providence had many upper-class residences. A few of these have not only survived, they have been revived and restored. One such example is the Israel B. Mason House (1888) at 571 Broad Street, which has housed the Andrew Bell Funeral Home since 1937. The original occupant of this Queen Anne–style mansion was a prominent meatpacker who operated a slaughterhouse on Willard Avenue in Dogtown. (Courtesy of the authors.)

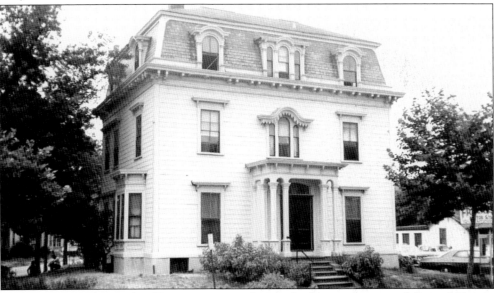

Andrew Comstock, another Dogtown meatpacker, built this nicely restored Second Empire mansion at 550 Broad Street in 1864. Andrew's brother and business partner, Jonathan, also built an elegant mansion (now demolished) on Broad Street at the opposite corner of a thoroughfare now called Comstock Avenue. The two Comstock houses were built by master carpenter Lorenzo Vaughn and were among the first houses built on Broad Street south of Trinity Square. (Courtesy of the Rhode Island Historic Preservation and Heritage Commission.)

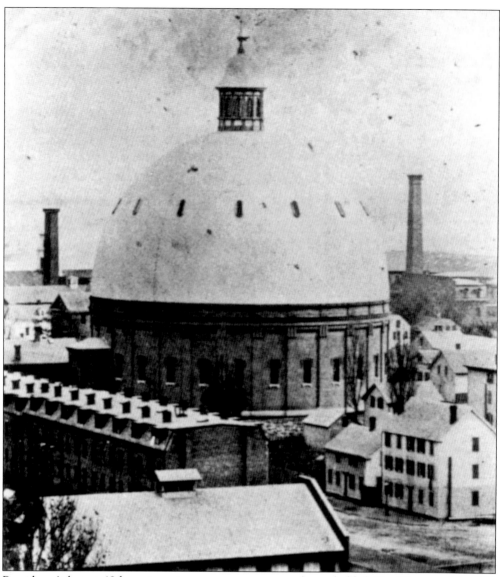

Providence's largest 19th-century structure was gasometer (or gasholder) No. 10, erected in 1872 between Crary, Hospital, and Borden Streets, just north of Rhode Island Hospital. The structure, 201 feet 10 inches tall at its highest point, dominated the Upper South Providence skyline. The outside diameter of the dome (136 feet) was nearly as large as the dome of St. Peter's in Vatican City (148 feet), but it was metal, not marble. The gasometer had become both an eyesore and a hazard (the city called it a "menace") when it was finally demolished in 1938. (Courtesy of the authors.)

Two

BURGESS COVE, DOGTOWN, AND THE EXPANSION OF SOUTH PROVIDENCE
1837–1906

Until 1731, the town of Providence included all of present-day Providence County west of the Blackstone River. By 1765, it had shrunk to less than six square miles because the Rhode Island General Assembly incorporated its "outlands" as separate towns. Cranston was set off in 1754, but in 1868, Providence took a chunk back that included South Providence. This reannexation extended from Dudley Street (the old city line) to the present boundary at Montgomery Avenue. This map by John Hutchins Cady details the process of reannexation. (Courtesy of the authors.)

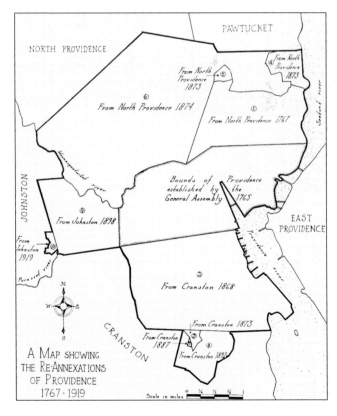

A MAP SHOWING THE RE-ANNEXATIONS OF PROVIDENCE 1767-1919

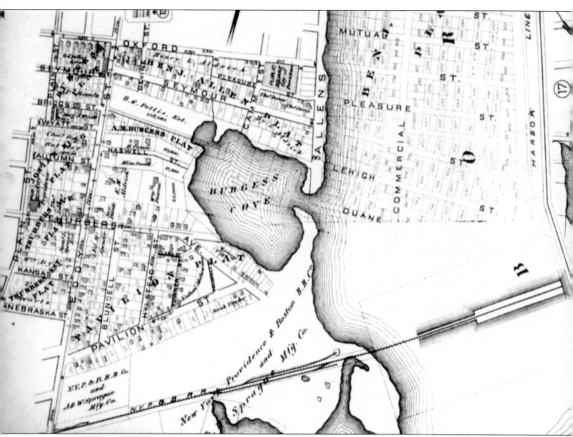

The Burgess Cove neighborhood was located in Cranston prior to 1868. Its riverfront site was made accessible by rail as well as by water in 1837 with the completion of the Providence-to-Stonington railroad. A small settlement developed here to accommodate rail traffic. It was capped by the Pavilion Hotel, which stood on a bluff overlooking the cove. The hotel was destroyed by fire in 1857, but it gave Pavilion Avenue its name. The cove was filled early in the 20th century to accommodate the widening of Allens Avenue and the industrialization of the waterfront. (Courtesy of the authors.)

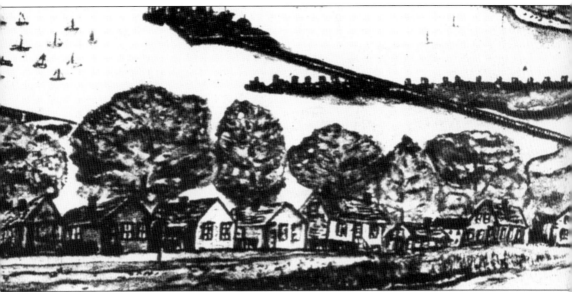

The initial Burgess Cove settlement stagnated temporarily when the railroad moved its terminus to Hill's Wharf at the foot of Lockwood Street and then to Union Passenger Depot in the city's center. In the 1850s, it experienced a revival after the extension of Thurbers Avenue to the river. Thurbers had a dogleg angling toward the southeast along the cove that acquired the name of Kay Street in 1891. Kay Street soon became known locally as "Rotten Row." This was a compliment rather than an insult. The name was conferred upon Kay Street by a pastor of St. Michael's Church who declared that its residents were so generous in their donations that he felt as if he were soliciting on Rotten Row, one of the most exclusive residential avenues of London. This 1893 watercolor by Robert Howard depicts Rotten Row with the Harbor Junction Pier in the background. (Courtesy of the Wentworth family.)

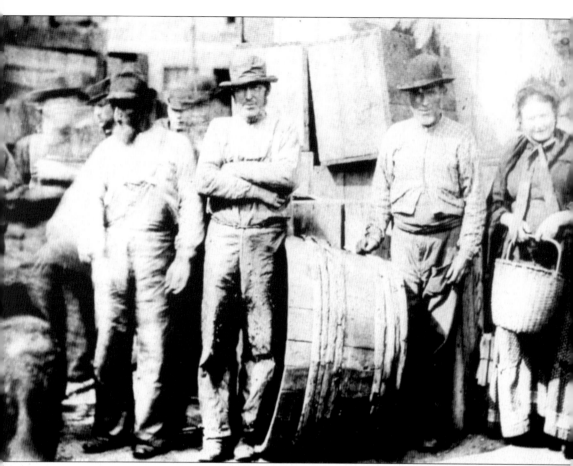

Irish immigrant workers from Dogtown take a break from their tasks at the Rhode Island Bleachery on Eddy Street near Dudley Street in this rare 1860 photograph. The dutiful wife of one worker has furnished the men with lunch. In addition to the bleachery, Irishmen such as these found work in one of Dogtown's four slaughterhouses located around Clinton Street (now Willard Avenue). Cattle, sheep, and hogs were driven to these malodorous establishments along Prairie Avenue for the last rites. "Hoardes of stray mongrels," says one recollection, feasted on the scraps of the animals that had been butchered—hence the pejorative name "Dogtown" was affixed to this Irish settlement. By the late 1860s, the slaughterhouses had relocated to Providence's North End. (Courtesy of the Providence City Archives.)

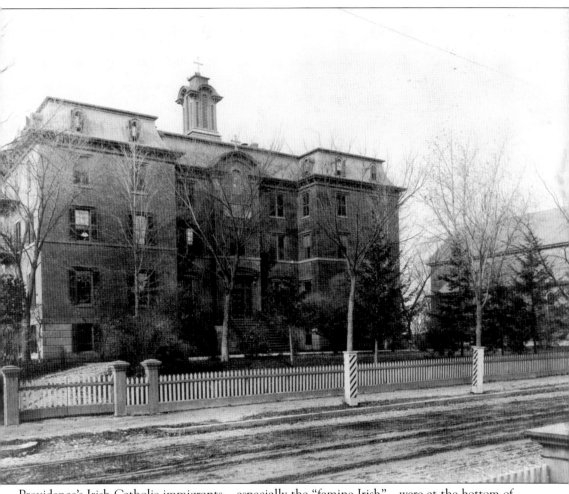

Providence's Irish Catholic immigrants—especially the "famine Irish"—were at the bottom of the city's socioeconomic ladder. Hazardous conditions of work, malnutrition, and unhealthful housing were often their lot. When epidemics struck, they hit the lowly hardest. For example, when cholera ravaged Providence in 1854 for the sixth successive year, 159 deaths from this scourge were recorded from May through September. Of these, 126 were Irish. Small wonder that an orphanage—eventually named St. Aloysius—was among the earliest social agencies created by the Catholic diocese. It was originally quartered in the convent of the Sisters of Mercy at Broad and Claverick Streets, where St. Xavier's Academy was also established, but it soon outgrew its original home. A decade after its founding in 1851, St. Aloysius moved to the spacious and modern building shown here on Prairie Avenue in the newly established St. Michael's Parish (then in the town of Cranston). When this structure was demolished in the late 1940s, the orphanage moved to Greenville. Note the Sister of Mercy peering out of the third-floor window. (Courtesy of the authors.)

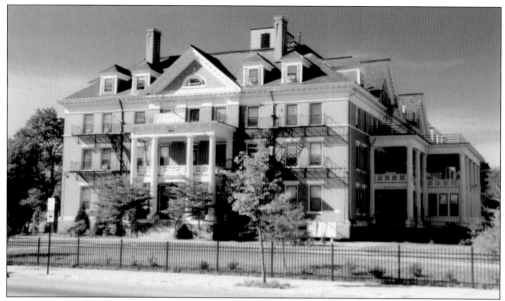

The Home for Aged Men was one of the earliest institutions that called South Providence home. It was established at 64 Point Street in 1874 and eventually moved to this spacious building at 807 Broad Street in 1895 through the generosity of Henry J. Steere, the president of Wanskuck Mills. Its purpose was soon expanded to accommodate aged couples, which it did until 1992. Today the building houses neighborhood social agencies, including the Rhode Island Indian Council. (Courtesy of the authors.)

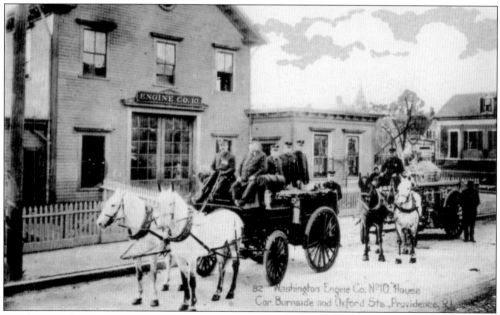

As the population of South Providence expanded, so did the need for safety services. Fire stations were built on Public, Broad, and Oxford Streets. Shown here on this 1906 postcard are the apparatus and personnel of Engine Company No. 10, located at the corner of Oxford and Burnside Streets. The station boasted a new Metropolital steam engine (right) and a hose wagon. (Courtesy of the authors.)

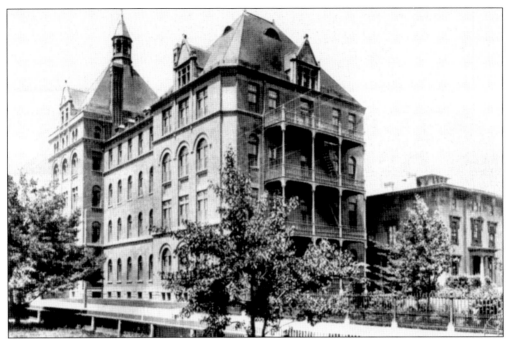

Bishop Matthew J. Harkins and Rev. William E. Stang (later the first bishop of Fall River) combined to establish St. Joseph's Hospital in 1892 in the former Harris homestead (right) on Broad Street, between Peace and Plenty Streets. The hospital's initial purpose was care of incurables, but its mission soon expanded to include general medical, surgical, and maternity care. The hospital was originally placed under the care of the Sisters of St. Francis, who were the first nurses. To supplement their ministrations, a home and school for nurses were erected on Peace Street in 1913. St. Joseph's offered convenient health care to the people of South Providence, especially its Irish Catholic community. Shown here is the hospital's original building. (Courtesy of the authors.)

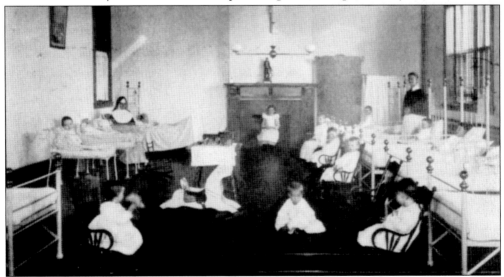

St. Joseph Hospital's annual report for 1897 (from which this photograph of the children's ward is taken) disclosed that the hospital cared for 775 children as ward patients and 357 as outpatients. The leading outpatient malady was malaria. (Courtesy of the authors.)

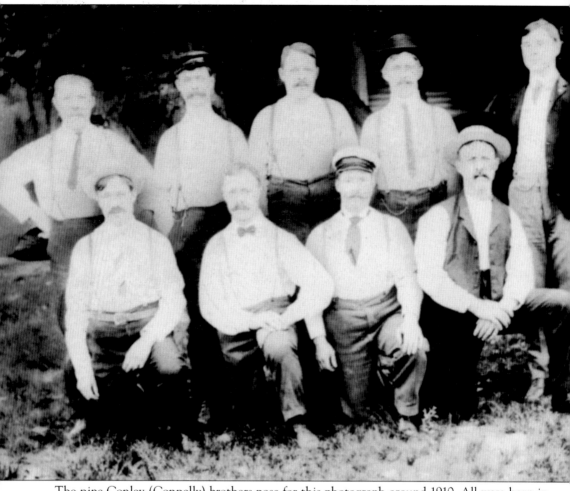

The nine Conley (Connelly) brothers pose for this photograph around 1910. All were born in Connemara, County Galway, and migrated from Ireland to South Providence in the late 19th century. Their parents, John and Mary Barrett Connelly, were brought out to America in the 1890s by their son Patrick after he had established himself in the gold refining business. Shown here, from left to right, are (first row) Joseph, Coleman, Thomas, and John J.; (second row) Patrick, Michael, Martin, James, and Austin. The family settled on Bishop (now Borinquen) Street in Dogtown. Their uncle, Thomas, married Irish immigrant Bridget Connelly (no relation) in 1873 and eventually set up house on Burgess Cove (25 Kay Street). The two Conley lines (those of John and Thomas) have been traced by Julia V. Conley (née Maney), whose 1990 genealogy lists 678 family members. (Courtesy of Julia V. Conley.)

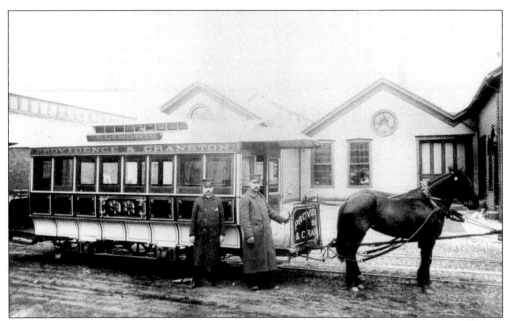

The Providence-Cranston horsecar traveled along Broad Street from downtown to Pawtuxet. The construction of this line in the 1860s gave rise to a phenomenon historians call "streetcar suburbs." These were outlying neighborhoods, like Lower South Providence, that could now be reached and settled. By 1894, the electric trolley had made horsecars obsolete. (Courtesy of Scott Molloy.)

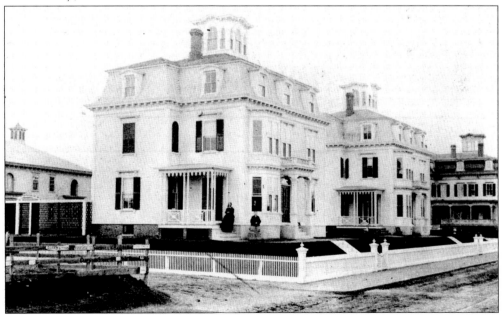

Eddy Street, originally called the Pawtuxet Turnpike, also boasted several impressive late-19th-century homes. Shown here are the George A. Rickard House (1872) at 865 Eddy Street (corner of Swan Street) on the left, and the Edwin A. Briggs House (1872) next to it on the right. Rickard was a grocer, and Briggs was a fruit and confectionery merchant. Only the Rickard House survives. (Courtesy of the Rhode Island Historical Society.)

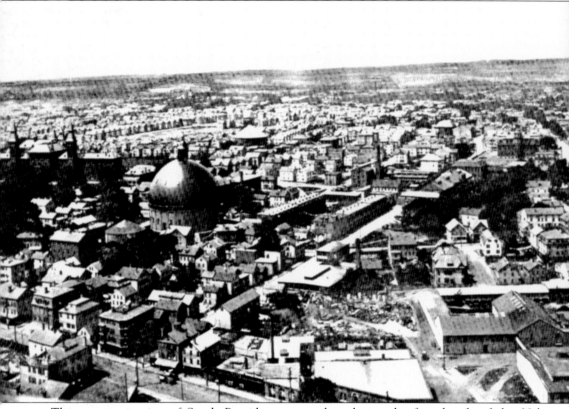

This panoramic view of South Providence was taken during the first decade of the 20th century, allegedly from the chimney of the Narragansett Electric Works. Since the Crary Street gasometer—201 feet 10 inches high—is well below the camera's eye, perhaps the vantage point was the basket of a balloon. The towers of Rhode Island Hospital can be seen at the left of the photograph, while Dogtown is in the center. This view serves to illustrate how densely populated South Providence had become since the 1850s. (Courtesy of Robert O. Jones Jr.)

Three

THE HEYDAY OF
THE NEIGHBORHOOD
1906–1968

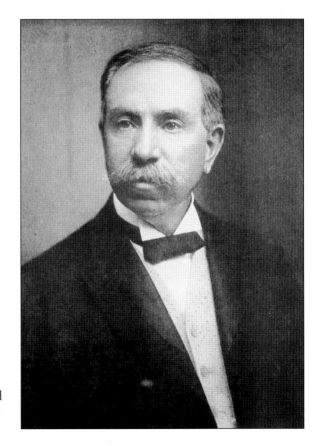

South Providence and its Dogtown sector gained a measure of respect in 1906 when Patrick J. McCarthy was elected mayor. McCarthy was not born in Dogtown but in County Sligo, Ireland. He was brought to Boston by his parents during the Great Famine migration. They died in quarantine, so their infant son entered America as an orphan. After receiving the equivalent of a high school education in Cambridge, Massachusetts, McCarthy moved to Dogtown in 1868, did readings in law, and earned sufficient funds in real estate to enroll at Harvard University Law School, from which he graduated in 1876. After serving the neighborhood as a Democratic councilman and state representative, he won two terms as mayor (1906 and 1907) before resuming the practice of law. (Courtesy of the authors.)

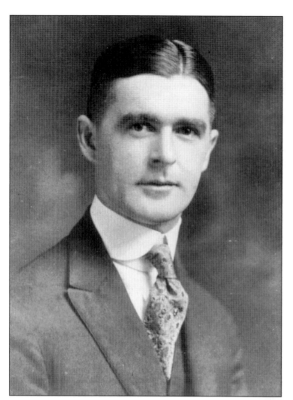

William S. Flynn, a Dogtown native and the son of a 5th Precinct cop, served as state representative from South Providence from 1912 to 1914 and from 1917 to 1922. He was elected Democratic governor of Rhode Island in 1922 and served one tumultuous term as a reformer before making an unsuccessful bid for the U.S. Senate in 1924. Flynn financed his education at Holy Cross College and Georgetown University Law School by working as a ticket agent for a Providence steamboat line. He resided at 252 Rhodes Street. (Courtesy of the authors.)

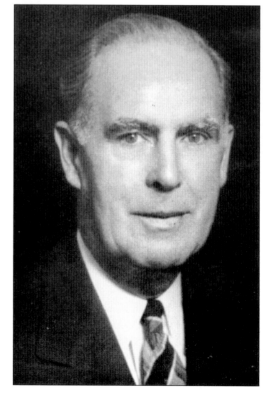

Edmund W. Flynn, the younger brother of the governor and of Jack Flynn, a major-league ballplayer, earned distinction in his own right. After graduation from Holy Cross College and Georgetown University Law School, he served five years as a Democratic state representative from South Providence. Flynn was elevated to the position of chief justice of the Rhode Island Supreme Court on January 1, 1935, as part of the famed "Bloodless Revolution." Known as a legal craftsman, Flynn died in office on April 28, 1957, as the longest-tenured chief justice in Rhode Island history. (Courtesy of the authors.)

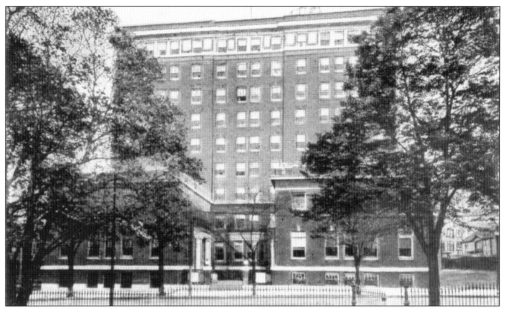

In 1913, the YMCA constructed an impressive nine-story hotel-type building at 160 Broad Street at the northeast tip of South Providence. It served as a residence and as a recreation center for the Protestant population of the neighborhood and offered a wide array of sporting activities, especially swimming, basketball, and track. In 2005, Crossroads Rhode Island, a social agency dedicated to assisting the homeless, took over the building as the YMCA announced plans to construct a new facility on the former site of the Gorham Manufacturing Company. (Courtesy of the authors.)

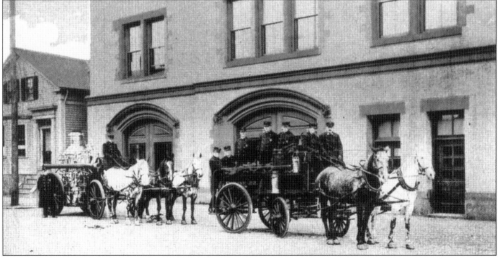

The Point Street fire station of Engine No. 22 was opened in 1908 and housed a ladder company (pictured above) as well as a first-size Metropolitan built by the American LaFrance Fire Engine Company of Elmira, New York, and a combination wagon built by J. G. McIntosh and Son of Providence. The station had a gymnasium on the third floor that in later days served as a center for departmental boxing and wrestling contests and as a Catholic Youth Organization boxing venue operated by promoter Leo Hunt. This station house was demolished in 1971. (Courtesy of the authors.)

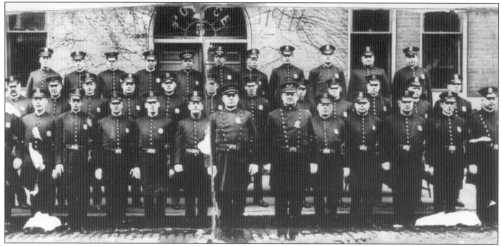

This 1916 photograph depicts the force of the 5th Precinct in front of police headquarters on 111 Plain Street. From 1886 to 1948, cops from this station patrolled the South Providence beat. (Courtesy of the Providence Police Department.)

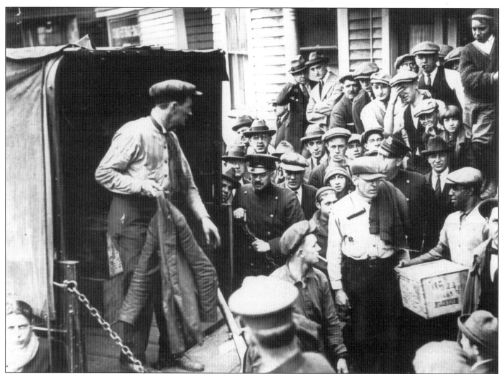

In 1919, the 18th Amendment was adopted, but no thanks to Rhode Island. Not only did the Rhode Island General Assembly vote against ratification, it also instructed the attorney general to challenge Prohibition's legality. Such protests were unavailing, and so the Providence police, sometimes reluctantly, cracked down on bootleggers (as the violators of Prohibition were called) in raids such as the one depicted here on Dogtown's Gay Street in 1924. Eventually the nation came to see the wisdom of Rhode Island's position. On December 12, 1933, Prohibition was repealed by the adoption of the 21st Amendment. (Courtesy of the Providence Journal.)

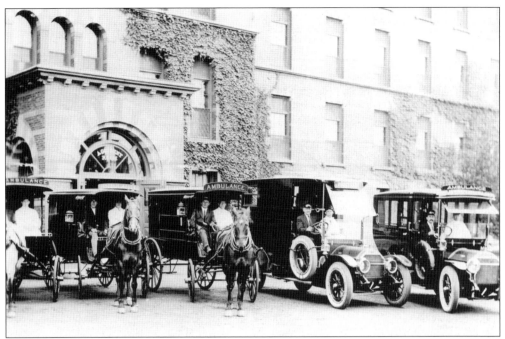

This early-20th-century image of the Rhode Island Hospital's ambulance corps graphically depicts its transformation from one kind of horsepower to another for its emergency vehicles. The Providence Fire Department made the same transition. At its height in 1911, the fire service stabled 120 horses. Nine years later there were none. (Courtesy of the Rhode Island Historical Society.)

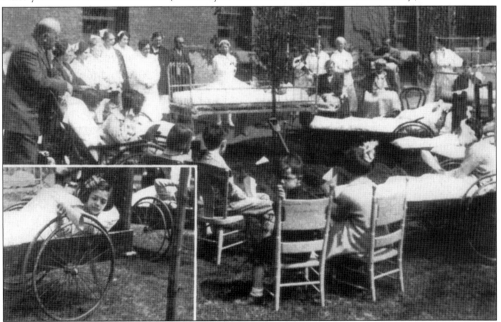

On May 12, 1932, the staff of Rhode Island Hospital conducted an Arbor Day observance at the children's ward. According to the hospital's annual report, "To this little patient fell the honor of pouring the first earth on the roots of the newly acquired tree." (Courtesy of the Providence City Archives.)

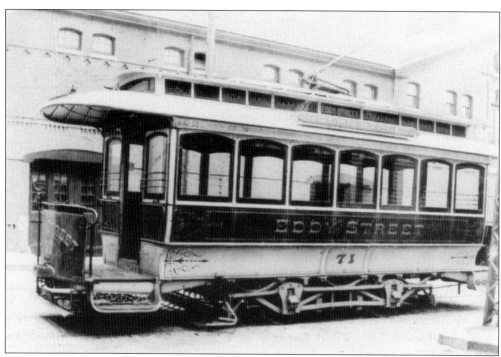

During the 1920s, residents of South Providence boarded conveyances like these to make their way to and from downtown. Above is the Eddy Street trolley, and below is the Metropolitan Rapid Transit Company's bus to Pawtuxet via Broad Street. This vehicle has been described as Providence's first motor coach. (Above, courtesy of Scott Molloy; below, courtesy of the authors.)

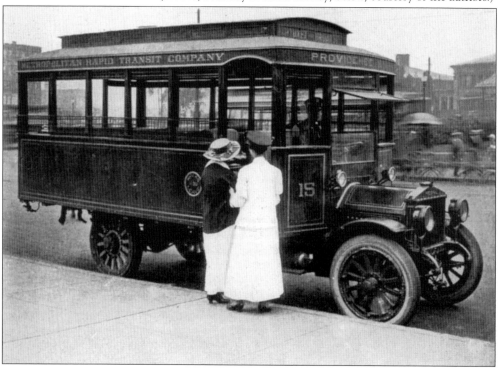

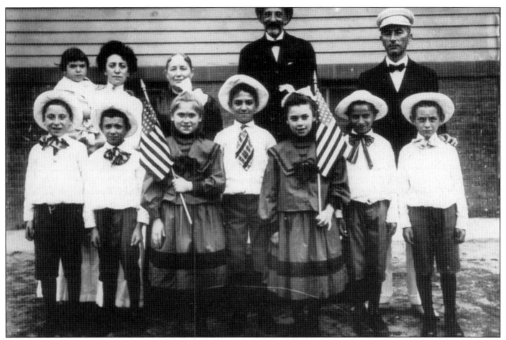

The Jewish community was an integral part of South Providence during its heyday. By the first decade of the 20th century, Jewish residents had assumed a strong presence in the old Dogtown area. One of the earliest surviving photographs depicting Jewish life in South Providence is this 1908 snapshot of the orphans and staff of the Machzeka Home for Jewish Orphans near the corner of Willard and Prairie Avenues. The flags and dress suggest a Fourth of July observance. (Courtesy of the Rhode Island Jewish Historical Association.)

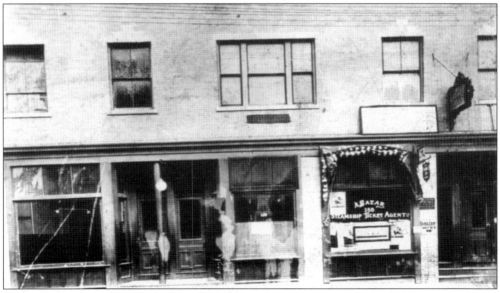

Built in 1908, Bazar's Hall at 161 Willard Avenue was a center of Jewish social life. Many weddings and dances were held here as were lectures and dramatic presentations. On Friday nights, the hall became the neighborhood's silent movie house. (Courtesy of the Rhode Island Jewish Historical Association.)

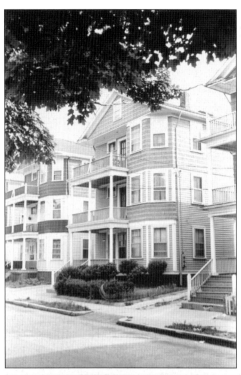

Three-decker houses, like these on Gordon Avenue, became the prevailing housing stock throughout South Providence. Benjamin Rakatansky had built 16 of these homes at 82–126 Gordon Avenue in the mid-1920s. Other Jewish entrepreneurs erected similar housing: Sigmund Rosen built 6 at 156–170 Dudley Street (1901–1906); Nathan Wiesel constructed 4 on Croyland Road (1907–1915); and Harry Weiss built 12 adjacent three-deckers on Thurbers Avenue, Meni Court, and Weiss Court. By the mid-1950s, many three-deckers were owned by the neighborhood's largest landlord—Isadore Schechtman. (Courtesy of the Rhode Island Historical Preservation and Heritage Commission.)

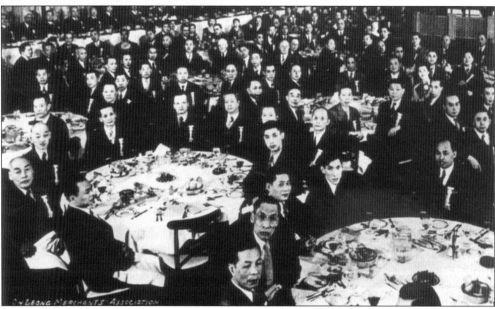

South Providence had a small but vibrant Chinese population confined by choice and prejudice to the area around Summer Street, Warner's Lane, and Graves Lane. The laundry and restaurant businesses were mainstays of the local Chinese families like the Chins, Moys, Wongs, and Tows. Their principal organization was the On Leong Tong, a national merchants association, whose local chapter was chartered on Empire Street in 1911. Providence's tong moved to Summer Street in 1914. This photograph of the association's regional convention was taken on Summer Street in 1936. (Courtesy of the Providence City Archives.)

Whereas 10th Ward Democrat Joseph F. Farrell of St. Michael's Parish presided over the common council from 1934 to 1936, 11th Ward Republican Henry "Mickey" Violet (right) of Cathedral Parish presided over the board of aldermen. The popular and charismatic Violet, who ran a gas station on Dudley Street and a parking lot, was a Republican in a Democratic stronghold. He was best known for the huge ice-cream parties he held each summer for neighborhood children and for his close relationship with Republican governor William H. Vanderbilt. Since the Democrats could not defeat him, Gov. J. Howard McGrath removed Violet from ward politics by appointing him to the state board of elections. (Courtesy of Henry E. "Buddy" Violet.)

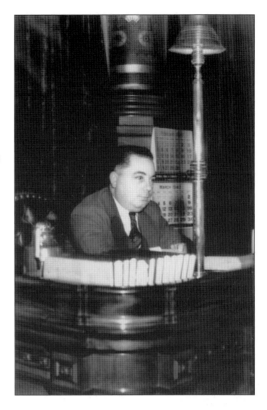

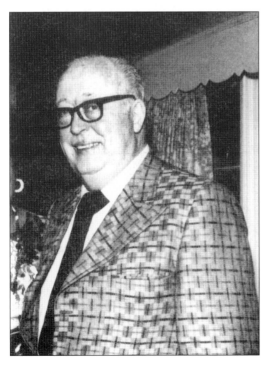

George E. Conley (1910–1979) was a man of great versatility. In his youth, he was an accomplished professional wrestler known as "Tiger Jack." He followed his uncle Patrick H. Conley, founder of Conley and Straight, into the gold refining business and owned Public Car Wash at the corner of Poe and Public Streets. George had a lifelong interest in politics, serving as state senator from Providence and running unsuccessfully as an unendorsed Democratic candidate for lieutenant governor and mayor of Cranston. He also held prominent positions in numerous business and civic organizations. (Courtesy of the authors.)

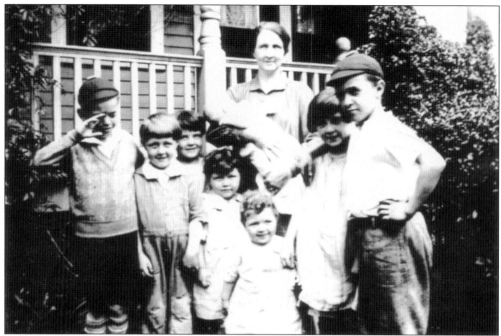

Mary Reilly of Thurbers Avenue proudly poses with the eight oldest of her nine children in the early 1930s during the depths of the Great Depression. Large families like the Reillys were not uncommon in South Providence. What was extraordinary about this family was the fact that Mary raised her offspring alone after the death of her husband, Frank. One of her children, Daniel (third from left), became the bishop of the Dioceses of Norwich and Worcester. (Courtesy of Bishop Daniel Patrick Reilly.)

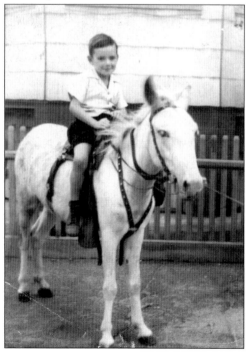

Many inner-city children got an opportunity to emulate their favorite cowboy—Tom Mix, Roy Rogers, Gene Autry, or the Lone Ranger—when a traveling photographer appeared on their street with his pony. The urban cowboy in this 1944 image is Thomas Dorsey of Trask Street. In the 1970s, he ran Dorsey's Tavern in Warwick in association with fellow South Providence chums Hank Johnson, Eddie Rodgers, and Ed Foster. This bar, over which Dorsey gradually assumed full ownership, was a reunion spot for those former South Providence residents who had moved to the West Bay suburbs. Dorsey eventually became a Providence County deputy sheriff (without the horse) and a leading benefactor of St. Michael's Parish. (Courtesy of Thomas Dorsey.)

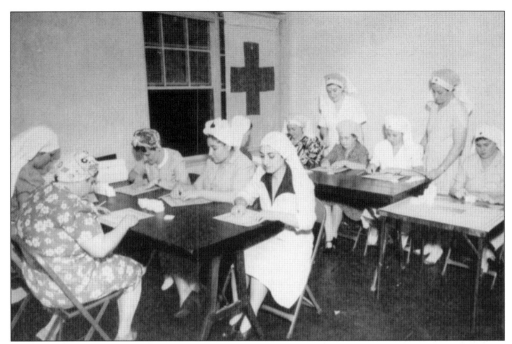

During World War II, many women who were not part of the regular workforce joined war-related volunteer agencies such as the United Service Organizations and the Red Cross, the latter of which prepared tons of surgical dressings and other medical supplies. Shown here are tenant volunteers from the Roger Williams Housing Project doing their part in this all-out war effort. (Courtesy of the Providence Housing Authority.)

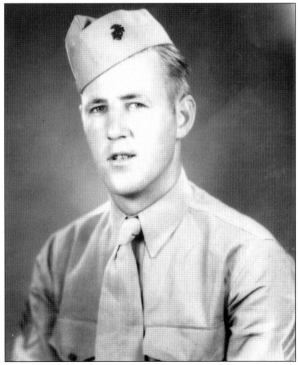

James and Delia Conley had four sons who served on active duty in World War II—James, John, Thomas, and Joseph. Of this four-star quartet, Joseph (right), nicknamed "Bucky," achieved the greatest local renown after sustaining a crippling wound on Iwo Jima. Bucky, a bona fide war hero, was affectionately called the "Mayor of South Providence." He was active in Democratic politics, and his military and political record earned him the appointment of U.S. marshal for Rhode Island, a post he held for five years. City High School Stadium in Mount Pleasant was renamed in his honor. (Courtesy of Serena and Joseph Conley.)

These are our boys. They once played in the streets of South Providence. No tribute payed to them would be more fitting, more thoughtful, and more to their way of wanting things to be than for us to make South Providence a better place, in all ways for their brothers and sisters.

Pvt. Nelson A. Alexander
S-Sgt. Hyman L. Banks
PFC. John J. Baynes
Pvt. Paul A. Bennett
2nd Lt. Leonard Bloom
PFC. Earle C. Bood
Capt. Everett J. Booth, Jr.
S-Sgt. Thomas A. Boyle
A-Rad. Arthur J. Breslin
Corp. George W. Brock, Jr.
PFC. William J. Brock
G-M Robert E. Budlong
C-MM Joseph M. Burns
Corp. Alfred J. Carmody, Jr.
1st Lt. Joseph W. Clampert
Pvt. William B. Cashman
Pvt. John P. Creegan
PFC. James E. Cronin
PFC. Albert M. Davis
Sgt. Richard P. Dawson
Pvt. William C. Devine
Sgt. Francis J. Dietz
S/1c Raymond J. Doherty
Pvt. Joseph Doyle
1st Lt. William S. Eichler
F/2c Frank A. Fantastia
Sgt. Raymond W. Flynn
PFC. John P. Ford
CM/2c Leslie R. Foss
Corp. Harry Friedenrich
QM/3c James J. Ganley
Pvt. James Gaul
Corp. William B. Gearey
Pvt. Oliver J. Gough

S/1c David F. Halpin
T/Sgt. Woodrow P. Harrison
S/2c Walter J. Hay
Sgt. Kenneth J. Heath
Pvt. Leonard J. Hodosh
Lt. Joseph A. Kayatta
Pvt. John L. Keaney
S/1c Milton R. Kee
Q/M/3 Gerald Kilberg
Pvt. John F. Langan
Phar/M/2c Edward F. Lyons
Pvt. Leo Ernest Martin
1st Lt. Harvey A. Max
Pvt. Herbert F. Moon
B/M/2 Ernest Allan Morey
Pvt. Lincoln P. Morton
Pvt. Lincoln P. Morton
Capt. John W. Mullaney
1st. Lt. Thomas A. Mulligan
PFC. William A. Mulvey
Lt. Edmund V. McDermott
M/M/2c John J. McGovern
A/Cadet William C. McLaughlin
S/Sgt. Vincent A. McMahon, Jr.
Pvt. Charles Nakshian
1st. Lt. James T. O'Brien
Arthur T. Pearson
Corp. Corwin D. Penoyer
PC. Edward R. Pina
2nd Lt. Joseph E. Szarko
2nd Lt. Thomas L. Toolin
PFC. George F. Wall
Pvt. James D. Wheaton
PFC. Richard W. Whipple
Pvt. Thomas C. White

World War II took a heavy toll on South Providence. Of the 2,157 Rhode Islanders who died in that conflict, the 69 men listed in this Providence Recreation Department commemorative booklet were from the South Providence neighborhood. Capt. Everett J. Booth Jr. and Capt. John W. Mullaney were the highest-ranking soldiers to die. The booklet was prepared in 1948 on the occasion of the dedication of Richardson Park to the memory of America's veterans. (Courtesy of Capt. Thomas E. Conley.)

Sgt. Raymond W. Flynn was one of the fighting 69 South Providence men to die in World War II. A resident of 391 Prairie Avenue, Flynn joined the Providence police force in 1938 and was assigned to Precinct 4 and then to the traffic division. He was granted a leave of absence on May 14, 1942, to serve in the U.S. Army. He rose to the rank of sergeant and participated in the Normandy invasion of June 6, 1944. Three days later, Flynn was killed in action. He was 33 years old. (Courtesy of the Providence Police Department.)

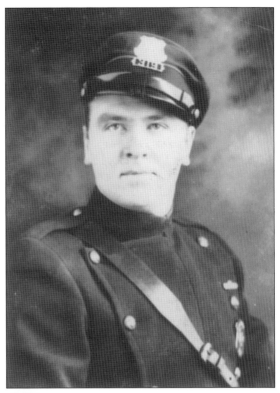

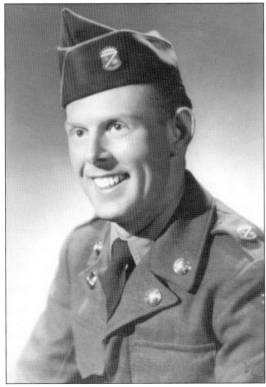

America's war in Korea produced its share of casualties and heroes. One of the latter was Cpl. Samuel J. Mullholland (left) of Ashmont Street, who joined the army with brothers Robert and Richard in November 1950. Samuel won the Bronze Star in 1952 for his part in "repelling an ambush of his patrol by numerically superior enemy forces." After the conflict, Samuel graduated from Rhode Island Radio School and the opened Mullholland Antenna and Communications Company at 757 Broad Street. The business moved to 1448 Fall River Avenue, Seekonk, in 1970, where it continues to operate. (Courtesy of Samuel J. Mulholland.)

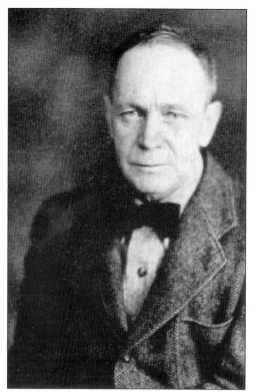

Relatively few neighborhoods or parishes have been the subjects of best-selling novels. South Providence and St. Michael's enjoy that distinction thanks to the literary efforts of Edward McSorley—newspaperman, publicist for movies, burlesque, and vaudeville, fisherman, and farmer. In 1946, Harper published McSorley's first novel—a 304-page work entitled *Our Own Kind*—which was advertised as "a deeply real and richly human novel of Irish-American life." McSorley spun the saga of Irish immigrant old Ned McDermott and his orphaned grandson Willie with South Providence as the setting and St. Malachi's (St. Michael's) as the center of the McDermotts' spiritual life. The work became a Book-of-the-Month Club selection. (Courtesy of the authors.)

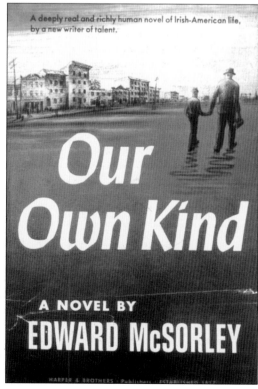

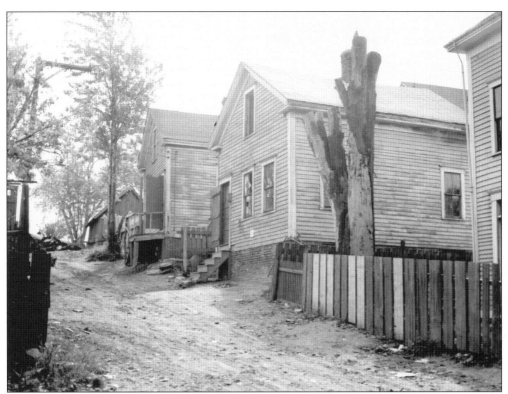

Other than the Social Security Act, the greatest social program of the New Deal was the National Housing Act of September 1937 (the Wagner-Steagall Act). Designed to improve housing conditions for low-income tenants, it created the U.S. Housing Authority, an agency authorized to extend low-interest, 60-year loans to local public authorities that provided at least 10 percent of the construction expense for low-cost housing projects built on marginal or slum-cleared land. Frog Hollow (top), a black ghetto near the junction of Pavilion Avenue and Rugby Street, fit that site description. Shanties like those shown here were demolished by the Providence Housing Authority (established in 1939), and Frog Hollow and its environs became the 744-unit, 28-building Roger Williams Homes. The project, shown below under construction, opened in 1943. The two 24-unit buildings on the site of Frog Hollow were assigned to blacks and Native Americans (such as the Guys and the Weedens). Here 48 families remained segregated until the mid-1950s. (Courtesy of the Providence Housing Authority and executive director Stephen P. O'Rourke of South Providence.)

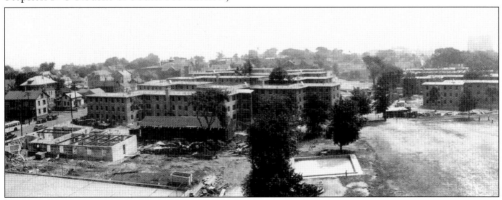

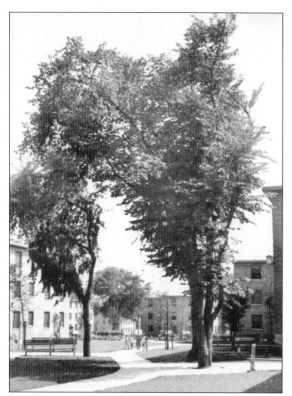

Roger Williams Homes was built for low-income families and defense workers at the Walsh-Kaiser Shipyard, and was eventually occupied by returning war veterans. The regimented blocks of buildings on pleasantly landscaped grounds (as shown here) were described by the state historic preservation commission as "an early experiment in garden apartment planning in Providence." In the 1950s, the residents of the project competed with one another to have their building be designated as "the most beautiful block." The project became a vandalized, crime-prone minority ghetto in the 1970s and was demolished in the 1980s, except for two refurbished 24-unit buildings on the southwest corner of the development. An elementary school and two specialized high schools now occupy a portion of the site. (Courtesy of the Providence Housing Authority and executive director Stephen P. O'Rourke.)

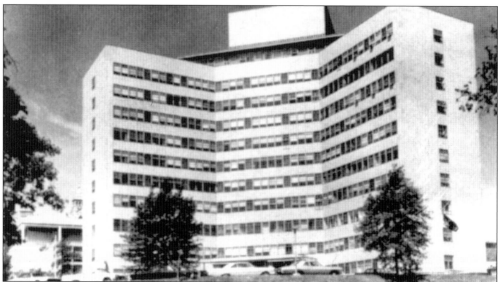

Rhode Island Hospital began its transformation into a modern medical complex in 1956 with the opening of this 10-story main building. Its construction resulted in the demolition of the original 1868 edifice. By 1970, the hospital had extended its boundaries north to Borden Street and across Plain Street to Beacon Avenue. In the 1980s, Women and Infants' Hospital joined the complex, whose boundaries now extend to Prairie Avenue on the west, Interstate 95 on the east, and Rhodes Street to the south. This institutional growth has dramatically altered the surrounding neighborhood. (Courtesy of the authors.)

John S. McKiernan, a graduate of Classical High School, Notre Dame University (cum laude, 1934), and Boston University Law School, became—ever so briefly—the second governor from South Providence. McKiernan was elected lieutenant governor in 1946 and held that post until May 7, 1956, when he accepted a position as associate justice of the superior court, except for a period of two weeks from December 19, 1950, to January 2, 1951, when he was governor of Rhode Island. His ascendancy was caused when Gov. J. Howard McGrath resigned to become U.S. attorney general. McKiernan filled in until governor-elect John O. Pastore was inaugurated. (Courtesy of the authors.)

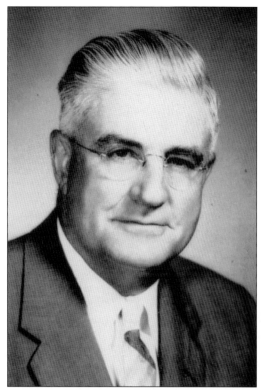

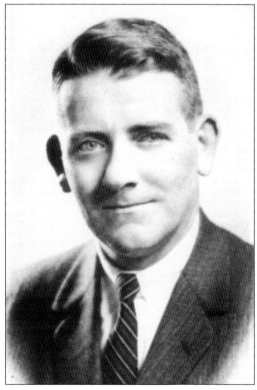

Edward P. Gallogly began his political career in 1957 as the state senator from South Providence. He served as lieutenant governor from 1961 to 1965 before losing a race for governor to incumbent John H. Chafee. Gallogly became U.S. attorney for the District of Rhode Island in 1967 and resigned to accept the position of chief judge of the family court. As the father of 11 children, Gallogly was well suited for his final public post. (Courtesy of the authors.)

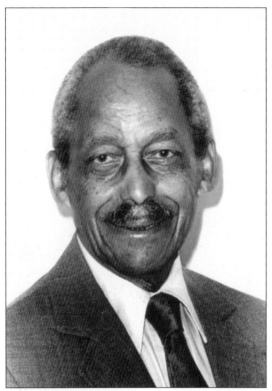

Andrew J. Bell Jr. was the leader of Providence's black community. In 1937, he established Bell Funeral Home in the former Israel Mason mansion at 571 Broad Street. It was and is the funeral home of choice for local African Americans. Bell's activities and importance went far beyond that of funeral director. He founded the Urban League of Rhode Island, served on innumerable public boards and commissions, and published a memoir prior to his death in 2000 relating to his experience as a black American in Rhode Island. (Courtesy of Dr. Jan Bell.)

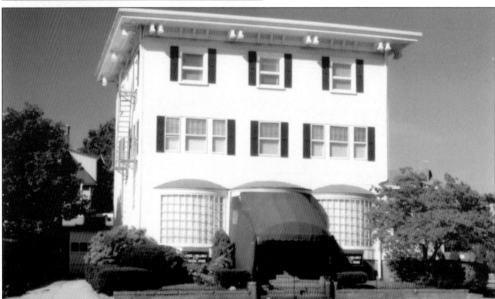

The James J. Gallogly and Sons Funeral Home is located at 671 Broad Street close to St. Joseph's Hospital. It was opened by the Gallogly family in 1929 and survived a serious fire in 1951. Its clientele at mid-century consisted mainly of Catholics from Upper South Providence. Although the Galloglys have maintained their South Providence base, they established a second funeral home at 5 Eddy Street, West Warwick, to be closer to the many former South Providence residents who resettled in the capital city's southern suburbs. (Courtesy of the authors.)

Frank P. Trainor and his two sons, Tom (left) and Ed, are depicted in front of the Trainor Funeral Home in this May 1949 image, taken shortly after the facility was established. The house, located at 859 Broad Street, was built by Jethro Hawes in 1897 and occupied from 1913 to 1944 by Dr. William McQuirk. For more than 37 years Trainor's was the last stop for the parishioners of St. Michael's Church. In 1978, the business followed its clientele to Warwick, where it now operates at 982 Warwick Avenue under the direction of Tom Trainor. The Providence home closed in 1984. (Courtesy of Tom Trainor.)

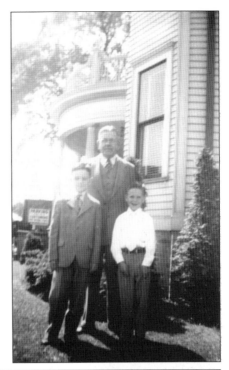

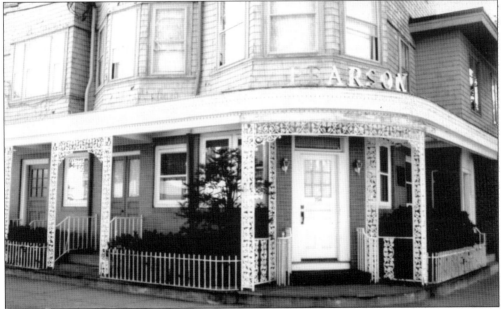

As Andrew J. Bell Jr. served the African American community and the Galloglys and the Trainors ministered to the Catholics of South Providence, the Juhlin-Pearson Funeral Home provided the final services for the local Protestant population and did so longer than any other neighborhood establishment of its kind. The home was founded on Prairie Avenue in 1899 and moved to 754 Broad Street in 1915, diagonally opposite from Calvary Baptist Church. Juhlin-Pearson continued to serve the needs of its South Providence neighbors until 2005 when it moved to East Greenwich. (Courtesy of the authors.)

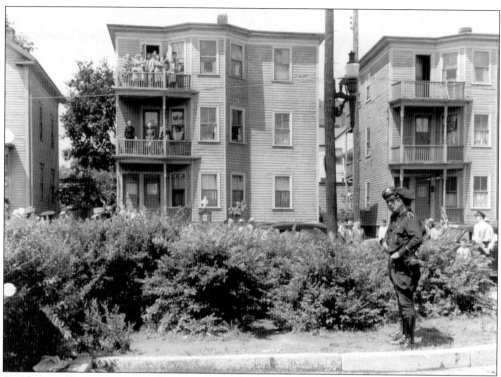

South Providence was a tough neighborhood, but murders were very rare. This crime scene photograph of Saturday, July 7, 1948, was taken adjacent to 628 Prairie Avenue in the Roger Williams Housing Project. The victim, Evelyn Burns, was found in the bushes by 10-year-old Patrick Conley. She had been raped and strangled en route home from a Friday night out. The Burns murder was never solved. (Courtesy of the Providence Police Department.)

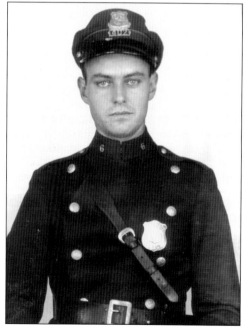

Young Walter McQueeney grew up on Houston Street within the shadow of St. Michael's Church. In October 1941, he became a patrolman for the Providence Police Department. Almost 30 years after this recruit photograph was taken in 1941, McQueeney became Providence's chief of police. During his career, he became an expert on narcotics and devoted himself to the battle against illicit drug traffic. He retired as colonel in 1976 and died a year later. McQueeney inspired three of his sons in their choice of careers—two became members of the state police and a third joined the Providence Police Department. (Courtesy of the Providence Police Department.)

Patrolman Robert Chin became Providence's first Chinese American policeman in 1974. Born in 1951, he was raised at 136 Summer Street during the final years of the neighborhood's Chinatown settlement. His parents operated the Far East Noodle Company, which supplied local Chinese restaurants. Chin was promoted to the detective division in 1984 and retired from the force 11 years later. He now serves as deputy chief of the Criminal Identification-Investigation Division of the Attorney General's Office. (Courtesy of Robert Chin.)

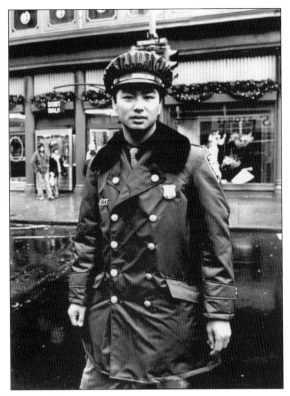

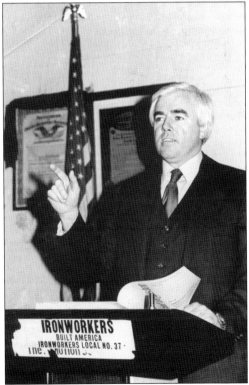

Marty Byrne, Billy Robinson, Charlie Healey, and Paulie Russell were tough, scrappy ironworkers who tried their hands, quite successfully, at professional boxing. Byrne (shown here) combined his brawn with brains. In 1958, he apprenticed as an ironworker and soon set his sights on gaining an education and becoming a labor leader. By 1969, he was elected the business agent for Ironworkers' Local 37. He also served as president of the Providence Central Labor Council, American Federation of Labor and Congress of Industrial Organizations (AFL-CIO), for 10 years before going to Washington, D.C., where he eventually assumed the post of executive assistant to the general president of the National Ironworkers Union. (Courtesy of William H. Byrne.)

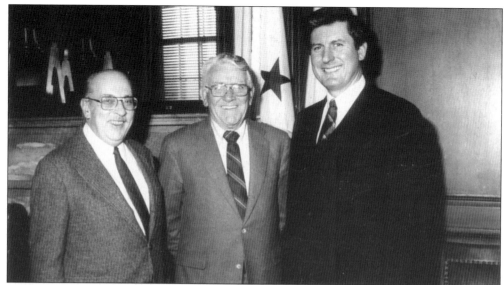

South Providence produced more than its share of judges. Here Edward V. Healey Jr. (left) and Edward P. Gallogly (center) pay tribute to neighbor and protégé Frank Darigan upon his appointment as district court judge on January 30, 1984. Healey, a graduate of Providence College and Boston University Law School, won the Bronze Star and other combat medals in World War II. One of the original justices of the family court, Healey served on that tribunal for nearly four decades. Darigan, former president of the diocesan Catholic Youth Organization and the Providence College student body, lost three bids for mayor of Providence after distinguished service on the city council. He performed so well at the district court level that he was elevated to the superior court in June 1991. (Courtesy of Frank Darigan.)

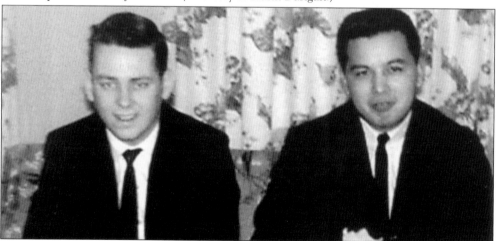

These two South Providence buddies also carved out careers in the state court system. Joe Rodgers (left) celebrates his 1962 graduation from Providence College with neighbor Jimmy Ham. Today Ham works in the superior court's Office of the Jury Commissioner, while Rodgers serves as presiding justice of the Rhode Island Superior Court. He ascended to that position in June 1991 after representing South Providence in the senate for seven years, holding a district court judgeship, and serving as an associate justice of the superior court from November 30, 1976. Judge Rodgers is the longest-tenured presiding justice in the 100-year history of the superior court. (Courtesy of Frank Darigan and Phyllis Warner [née Marshall].)

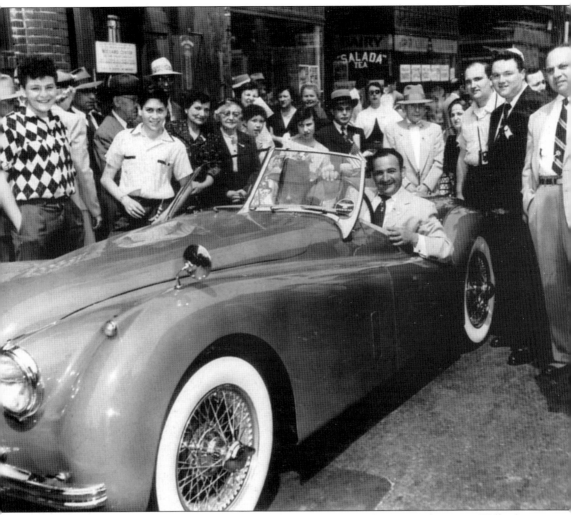

Young Jake Kaplan of Dudley Street displays his new Jaguar to an admiring audience on Willard Avenue in this 1956 photograph. Kaplan began his automotive career as the owner of Trinity Auto Sales on Trinity Square. He was a sports-car enthusiast and often raced Jaguars and Alfa Romeos at Sebring, Watkins Glen, and other race courses. By the time of his death in 1991, Jake Kaplan's name had become synonymous with Jaguar. He built a stylish showroom on Elmwood Avenue, not far from Trinity Square, and had the city rename the abutting street Jake's Way. He also engaged in a large-scale neighborhood restoration effort in the vicinity of his dealership. (Courtesy of the Rhode Island Jewish Historical Association.)

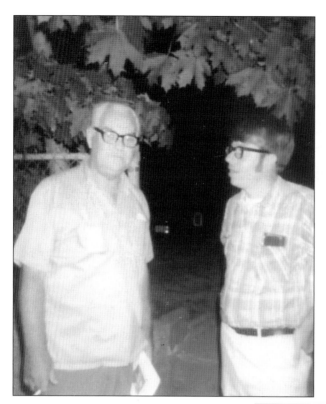

Council majority leader Joseph P. McNulty (left), a teacher at LaSalle Academy, is shown campaigning with fellow 10th Ward councilman Donald E. McKiernan in this 1970 photograph. On November 21, 1970, shortly after winning reelection for his sixth term, McNulty died of a heart attack and was succeeded by Harry A. "Buddy" Johnson, who won a special election for the post on February 16, 1971. McKiernan, also a teacher, was a brilliant political strategist and a specialist in economic policy. He went on to become the city treasurer of both Providence and Warwick and chief fiscal adviser to Congressman Robert O. Tiernan and the Rhode Island Senate. (Courtesy of Donald E. McKiernan.)

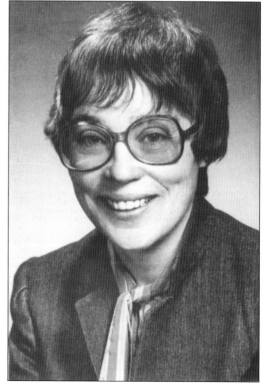

Arlene Violet is the daughter of alderman Mickey Violet, and the apple did not fall far from the tree. She gained her education in the Upper South Providence fashion at Tyler School and St. Xavier's Academy before earning a bachelor of arts degree from Salve Regina University. She entered the Sisters of Mercy, but after earning a law degree from Boston College while still a nun, Arlene decided she could be more of a force for change as a public figure. On November 6, 1984, running as a Republican, she became the first woman in America to win election as state attorney general. Today she is Rhode Island's most influential talk show host. (Courtesy of the authors.)

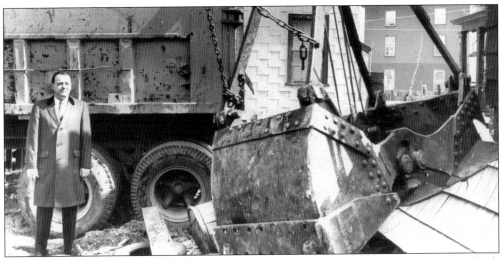

Upper South Providence was designated a Model Cities Area in 1967, making federal funds available there for slum clearance and for the neighborhood's reconstruction in the image of suburbia. Only the clearance program succeeded. Even before the infusion of Model Cities funding, the city took the initiative and launched a campaign to rid the area of hazardous structures. This April 7, 1966, image shows the razing of the first building in South Providence by the city, an occasion presided over by Mayor Joe Doorley (left). Between 1966 and 1979, more than 61 percent of all residential units in Upper South Providence were demolished. Lower South Providence experienced a similar reduction, and littered vacant lots actually outnumbered houses in this once densely populated neighborhood. (Courtesy of the Providence Journal.)

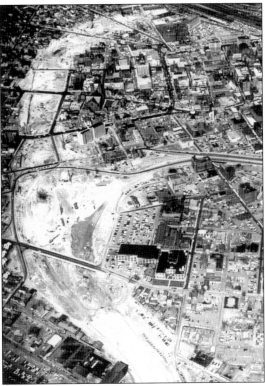

The crescent-shaped swath of vacant land on the left of this 1962 aerial photograph is not the path of a tornado. The scar left by the construction of Interstate 95 through South Providence was even more thorough and permanent than a mere storm. Point Street School, Tyler School, and Hayward Park, as well as a commercial district along Pine Street and Beacon Avenue, were eradicated, and the southern half of Byfield Street also vanished. Fortunately, the roadbed was diverted through the so-called "Badlands" between Eddy Street and Allens Avenue where little of value was lost. The completion of Interstate 95 in 1964 greatly shortened the commute time from the suburbs, thus facilitating migration from the inner-city neighborhood. (Courtesy of Lenscraft Photos, Inc., and the Providence City Archives.)

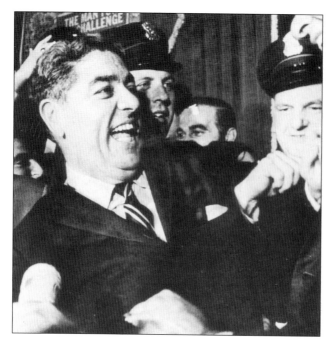

In November 1968, South Providence experienced its last hurrah (shown here) when its native son, Judge Frank Licht, upset popular incumbent John H. Chafee to become Rhode Island's first Jewish American governor. Born in 1916 at 21 Gay Street, this junk dealer's son graduated from Brown University (1938) and Harvard Law School (1941), before serving seven years as state senator from Providence's East Side and over 12 years as an associate justice of the superior court. The Providence County Court House, presided over by Joe Rodgers, was renamed the Licht Judicial Complex in Licht's honor. (Courtesy of the Providence Journal.)

Larry McGarry is best described as a shrewd and basically honest South Providence politician of the old school. Although he earned only a high school diploma (from LaSalle Academy), he possessed sound judgment and good political instincts that carried him from the post of Ward 10 committeeman to the city and the state Democratic chairmanships. McGarry obligingly poses for a *Providence Journal* photographer after masterminding the upset gubernatorial victory of Frank Licht over John H. Chafee on November 5, 1968. The butt-filled ashtrays were the witty chairman's response to allegations that he was a machine boss who made decisions in smoke-filled back rooms. As McGarry later remarked, "The political machine (so-called) is just ordinary people. . . . In all my years, I never saw anything dishonest take place in a back room." (Courtesy of the Providence Journal.)

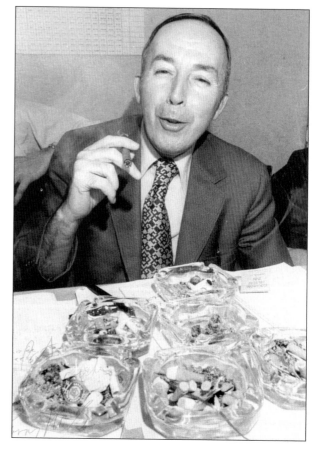

Four

THE WATERFRONT
IMMIGRANTS AND INDUSTRY

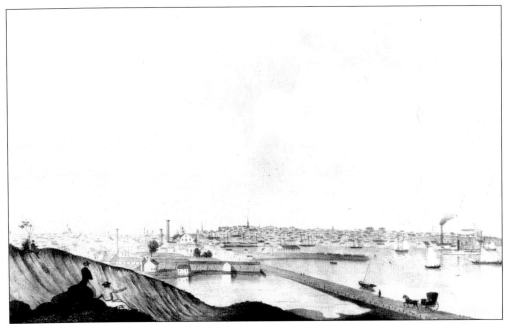

An excellent view of mid-19th-century Providence from the South Providence riverbank is furnished in this 1848 lithograph by Fitz Hugh Lane. The causeway across Hawkins Cove (center) approximates the route of present-day Allens Avenue. It carried the tracks of the Providence and Stonington Railroad to its station at the foot of Crary Street. The train route was altered in 1848 when Union Passenger Depot in the downtown became the line's new terminus. The buildings of the Rhode Island Bleachery (1838) and the Providence Machine Company (1846) are on the left beyond the cove. (Courtesy of the authors.)

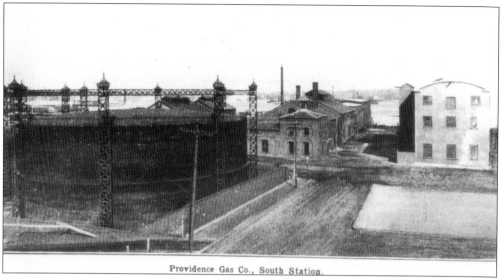

Providence Gas Co., South Station.

In 1899, the Berlin Iron Bridge Company built this purification plant (coal degasification facility) for the Providence Gas Company. Known as the South Station (right), it was operated by the utility until 1917. Thereafter, the structure had several uses. In 1940, City Tire Company began operations here that lasted for 60 years. In 2002, this historic structure—the oldest on Providence's outer harbor—was acquired by Patrick and Gail Conley. They renamed it Conley's Wharf because of its proximity to State Pier No. 1, renovated it (see below), placed it on the National Register of Historic Places, and converted it to artists' studios, a conference center, and Patrick's Pier One Function Facility. (Courtesy of the authors.)

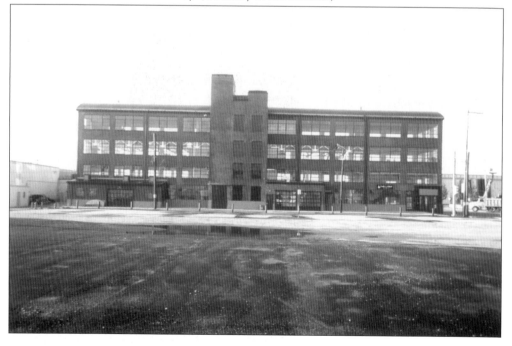

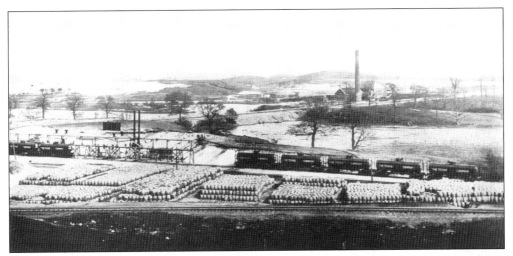

When this image was taken in 1908, Harbor Junction had become a heavily industrialized area, and its enlarged pier regularly received the tankers of the Texas Oil Company (Texaco). The oil and petroleum products were unloaded into railroad tank cars, like those shown above, and distributed throughout the region by rail. One of Texaco's dock workers was Patrick "Packy" Conley, who lived nearby at 25 Kay Street. Conley died in 1955, and Kay Street is now the site of a scrap metal yard, yet oil tankers still dock regularly at the Harbor Junction pier. (Courtesy of Julia V. Conley.)

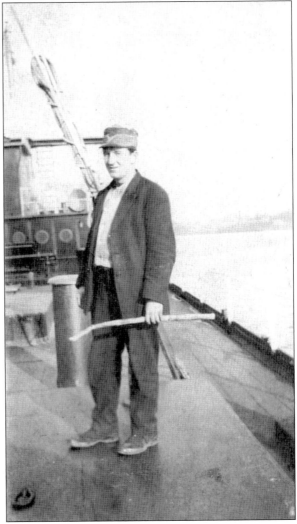

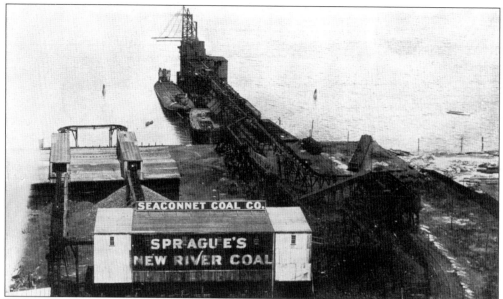

This is the earliest photograph (taken around 1905) of the Seaconnet Coal Company terminal of C. H. Sprague and Son (now called Sprague Energy). For its first half century, coal was the terminal's principal import. Colliers (coal carrying ships) docked to be unloaded by steam-operated cranes. There the coal was transferred to storage piles via a conveyor-trolley system. The transition of the terminal from coal to oil began in 1953 and was completed in 1968. (Courtesy of the Rhode Island Historical Society.)

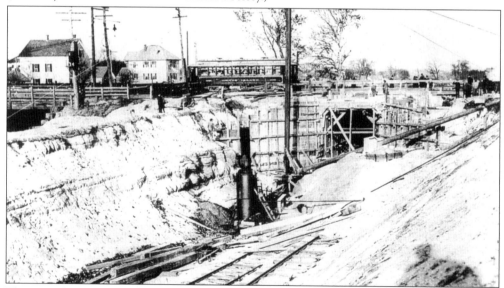

This 1912 photograph shows the construction of a tunnel under Broad Street parallel to the Harbor Junction tracks. The tunnel was designed to facilitate the passage of Grand Trunk Railroad cars to State Pier No. 1, then also under construction. Charles M. Hays, president of the Grand Trunk, a Canadian line, planned to make the port of Providence the Atlantic terminus of a transcontinental railroad network that could tap the trade of Canada. Unfortunately for Providence and the success of this grand scheme, Hays perished with the *Titanic* in 1912, prompting one writer to speak of "the railroad that perished at sea." (Courtesy of the Providence Journal.)

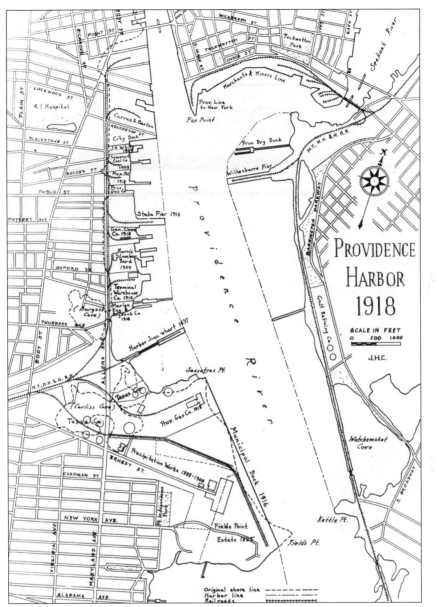

This detailed map of Providence Harbor was drawn by John Hutchins Cady to reveal the dramatic progress of port development from 1909 to 1918. In the former year, a government-sponsored commercial survey declared that the port of New York was overburdened and advised steamship companies to divert some of their tonnage to other ports. Providence geared up to take advantage of the situation with the assistance of the state, which floated bonds in 1909 and 1912 to finance the acquisition of waterfront property in Providence, East Providence, and Pawtucket. The federal government joined this partnership to upgrade the port, agreeing to match state and city expenditures, by dredging the entire harbor from Field's Point to Fox Point to a depth of 30 feet and a width of 600 feet. The result of these improvements was dramatic. Providence became a major immigrant landing station, especially for Italians and Portuguese, and the city developed into a leading regional distributor of oil from the Gulf of Mexico area and lumber from the Pacific Northwest. (Courtesy of the authors.)

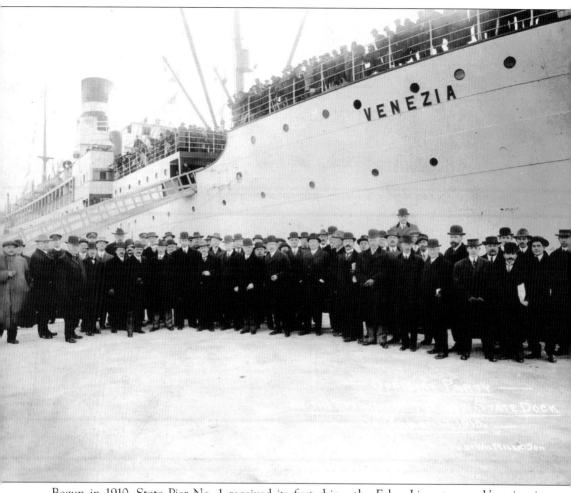

Begun in 1910, State Pier No. 1 received its first ship—the Fabre Line steamer *Venezia*—in December 1913. Here, dignitaries pose on the dock while Italian and Portuguese arrivals watch anxiously from the *Venezia*'s deck. Because the Fabre steamships made calls in Italy and Portugal en route from Marseilles, many immigrants from those countries came directly to Providence. The federal Bureau of Immigration kept detailed statistics from 1898 to 1932 on the ethnicity and destination of all aliens arriving in the ports of the United States. Those tabulations listed 54,973 Italians migrating to Rhode Island, the bulk of them to Greater Providence. Of these, 51,919 were from the south of Italy and 3,054 from the north. Portuguese designating the state as their destination in this 34-year span totaled approximately 20,000. Nearly all of these Italian and Portuguese arrivals bypassed South Providence, but the neighborhood developed two small Italian enclaves; one, just west of the pier and east of Eddy Street, contained families such as the Petrarcas, the Cornicellis, the Filuminas, the Celibertos, the Vinaccos, and the Vesceras, and a second, south of Point Street near Coro's, was home to the Voccios, the Carmones, the Squillantes, and the Giordanos. (Courtesy of the authors.)

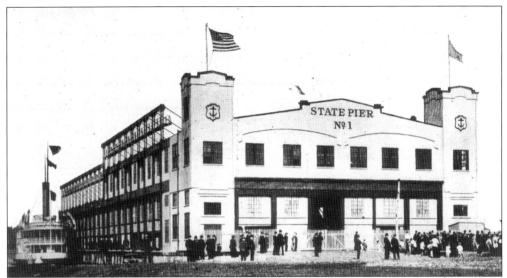

State Pier No. 1 was formally dedicated on May 21, 1914. The facility encompassed 17 acres of land and a two-story building—400 by 100 feet (shown here)—used for passengers, baggage, and freight. The pier burned in 1931 and was rebuilt. This facility was Rhode Island's Ellis Island. When the National Origins Quota Acts of 1921 and 1924 curtailed the volume of immigration from Italy and Portugal, the Fabre Line scoured the eastern Mediterranean and Black Sea for Greeks, Armenians, Syrians, Lebanese, Ukrainians, Romanians, and Russian Jews. With the exception of a small number of Greeks and the eight Ukrainian families that established St. John's Ukrainian Orthodox Church on Pilgrim Street in 1921, these groups did not settle in South Providence. (Courtesy of the authors.)

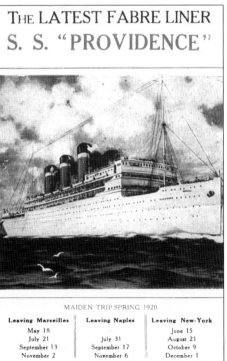

THE LATEST FABRE LINER
S. S. "PROVIDENCE"

MAIDEN TRIP SPRING 1920

Leaving Marseilles	Leaving Naples	Leaving New-York
May 18		June 15
July 21	July 31	August 21
September 13	September 17	October 9
November 2	November 6	December 1

The 11,996-ton SS *Providence* was the queen of the Fabre Line. When the vessel made its maiden voyage to the city in June 1920, bearing officers of the line from Marseilles, France, and the Portuguese minister to the United States, it was the largest ship to visit Providence up to that time. The Fabre Line—which sent its first vessel, the *Madonna*, to the city in May 1911—maintained service to Providence until July 1934. Incoming liners left Marseilles and made pickups at Naples and Palermo in Italy, Lisbon in Portugal, Madeira, and the Azores before discharging their passengers at State Pier No. 1, where the federal government had established an immigrant landing station. The *Providence* remained in service until 1951, when it was sold and scrapped. (Courtesy of the authors.)

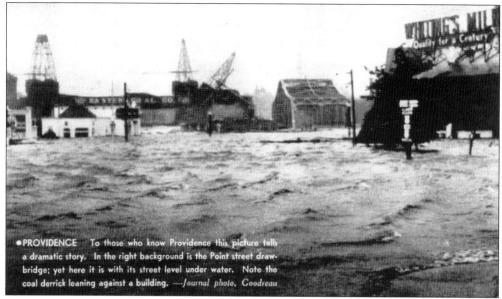

On September 21, 1938, Rhode Island's worst hurricane lashed the South Providence waterfront destroying docks, boats, and buildings. This picture was taken from Fox Point at the height of the storm. It shows that water levels had risen above the roadway on the Point Street Bridge. Eastern Coal Company at 70 Point Street (the present site of the National Grid Power Plant) sustained heavy damage. (Courtesy of the Providence Journal.)

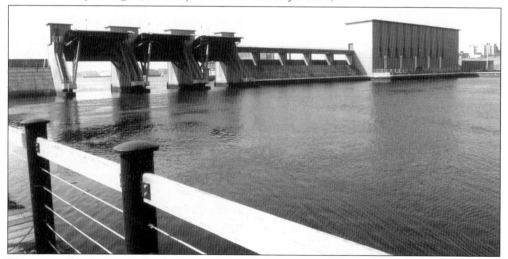

To prevent the disastrous flooding of downtown, such as occurred in 1815, 1938, and 1954, the Army Corps of Engineers conducted a study of the bay in 1955–1956 and recommended the construction of a hurricane barrier across the Providence River from Fox Point to the South Providence shore. Congress approved the project in April 1958, and in November 1960, Rhode Island voters passed a $1,750,000 referendum to provide the state's 10 percent of the barrier's cost. Another 10 percent was furnished by the city, and a third 10 percent contribution was made by property owners in the hurricane hazard area. M. A. Gammino won the contract and began work on the $18 million project in July 1961. The elaborate undertaking, with its gates extending across Allens Avenue on the west and to India Point on the east, took more than four years to complete. It was dedicated on March 19, 1966. (Courtesy of the authors.)

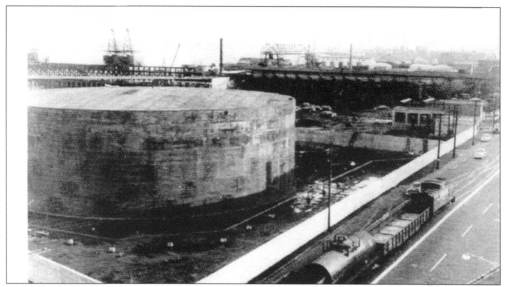

Freight trains were a common sight on Allens Avenue through the 1960s. The tracks, which ran down the center of the avenue, had numerous spurs to service the many large businesses along the route. The train depicted here is passing the Sprague Energy terminal. Its caboose was the domain of brakeman Larry Cahalan of Central Falls, a veteran on the Harbor Junction line of the New York, New Haven, and Hartford Railroad. His daughter, Gail, is now the codeveloper of a large site just south of Sprague known as Providence Piers. (Courtesy of Sprague Energy.)

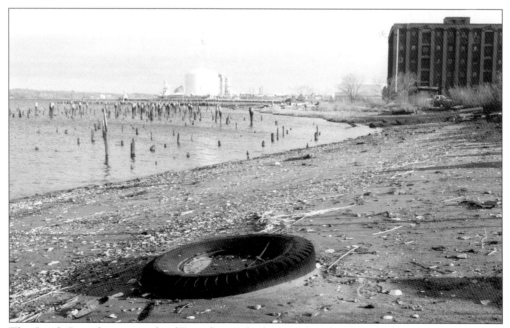

The South Providence stretch of Providence's harbor can best be described as a tired waterfront. The hurricanes of 1938 and 1954 dealt mortal blows to several businesses. The pilings of the piers destroyed by those hurricanes are still visible in this recent photograph. At the right is the run-down and nearly vacant Shepard warehouse, which dates from 1913. (Courtesy of the authors.)

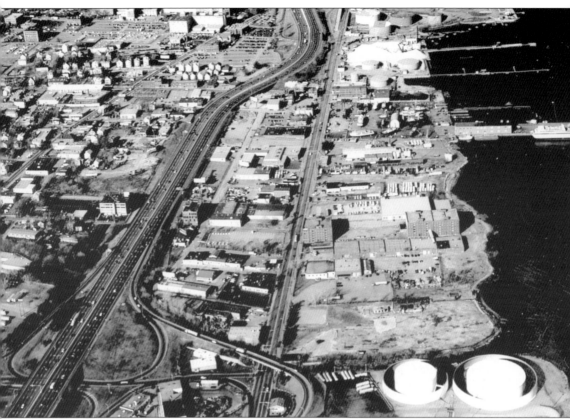

A large span of the South Providence waterfront (from Harbor Junction on the bottom, or south, to Franklin Square) is depicted in this photograph. Much of the waterfront land is vacant or underutilized. Note how Interstate 95 has separated the South Providence neighborhood from the river. (Courtesy of the authors.)

Five

SOUTHSIDE SPIRITUALITY
CHURCHES AND SYNAGOGUES

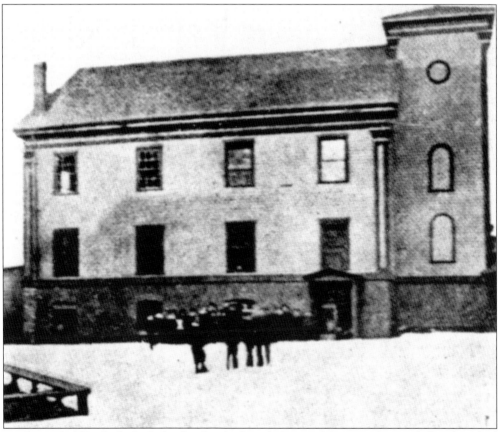

By the mid-1850s, Irish Catholic families had settled around Burgess Cove, while others had moved to the newly subdivided lands south of Dogtown. Since the distance to the Cathedral of SS. Peter and Paul was great, Msgr. William O'Reilly acquired a Baptist meetinghouse on Prairie Avenue near Oxford Street in 1857 and converted it to St. Bernard's Mission, named in honor of Bernard O'Reilly, the second bishop of the Diocese of Hartford (which then included Rhode Island). Bernard had died at sea in 1856 en route home from a recruiting trip to Ireland, where he had gone to entice priests, brothers, and nuns to his diocese. (Courtesy of the authors.)

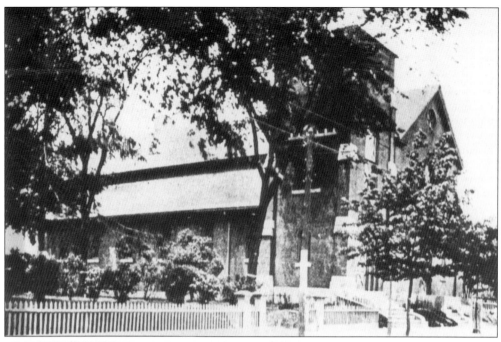

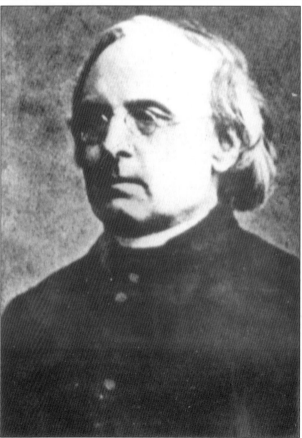

The Rev. Michael Wallace (left) was St. Michael's third pastor (Fr. Bernard Coit was the first). Wallace, a published poet, presided over his Irish immigrant flock for 28 years (1864–1892). He built a second church for his expanding congregation on Prairie Avenue in 1868 (above), dedicating it to his namesake, St. Michael the Archangel. That structure became the parish hall when the present church was completed. It was the venue for school minstrels and basketball games and the meeting place for the many parish societies until it fell victim to arson on New Year's Eve in 1969. (Courtesy of the authors.)

St. Ansgarius Swedish Episcopal Church, on Beacon Avenue adjacent to Hayward Park, exemplified the neighborhood's ethnic and religious diversity. It was established in 1886 and was one of five Swedish churches founded in Providence during the late 19th century. The other Swedish house of worship in South Providence had a Baptist affiliation. Located at the corner of Plain and Emmett Streets, it now contains medical offices. Other ethno-religious groups built churches just beyond the borders of South Providence, most notably the Greek Orthodox Church of the Annunciation. It was established on lower Pine Street in March 1921 and had a significant number of South Providence parishioners. (Courtesy of the authors.)

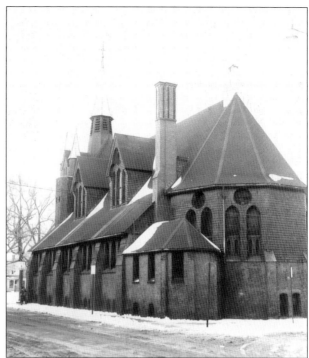

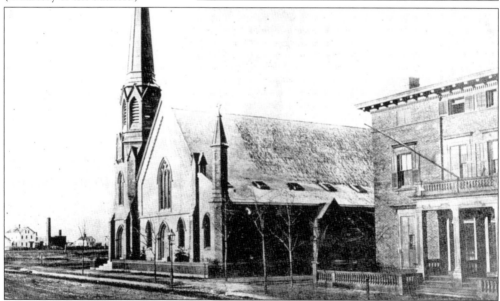

Trinity United Methodist Church, a Gothic Revival building, was completed in 1865 at the junction of Broad Street, Bridgham Street, and Elmwood Avenue, diagonally opposite historic Grace Church Cemetery. It drew its adherents both from South Providence and the Elmwood neighborhood. In the late 19th century, it had the largest congregation and Sunday school of any church in the Southern New England Conference of the Methodist Church. The intersection over which the church presided was named Trinity Square in 1875. Trinity also gave its name to Providence's famed repertory theater, which originated in the church's basement in 1964. (Courtesy of the Rhode Island Historical Society.)

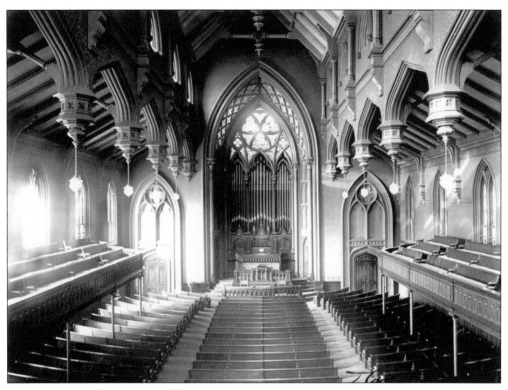

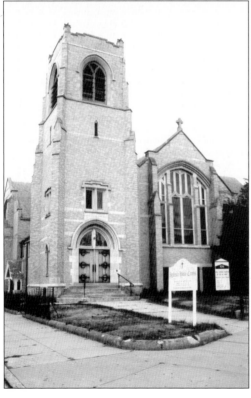

The Union Congregational Church (top) was a stately, twin-spired Gothic Revival building located on the northerly side of Broad Street between Summer Street and Stewart Street. The congregation formed in 1871 and completed its church in 1877. By the third decade of the 20th century, most of the worshipers had moved from Upper South Providence, so Union effected a merger with Plymouth Congregational Church in 1922. Its abandoned edifice was demolished in 1928. The Plymouth church, organized in 1878 in Lower South Providence, built its handsome English Gothic–style building (left) in 1915 at 1014 Broad Street, on the corner of Pennsylvania Avenue. The merged religious group operated as Plymouth Union Congregational Church for nearly five decades. By the early 1970s, however, most of its adherents had moved to the suburbs, and the building was sold to the Holy Cross Church of God in Christ. This group has conducted services there for more than three decades. (Courtesy of the authors.)

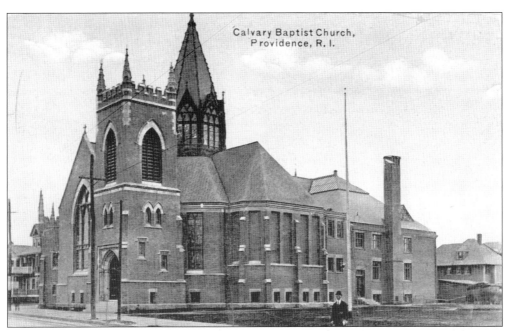

Calvary Baptist Church,
Providence, R. I.

Calvary Baptist Church (organized in 1854 as the Friendship Street Baptist Church) remains the Southside's most elegant and stately Protestant church building. Constructed in 1905–1907 at 747 Broad Street, just south of Public Street, it served residents of both South Providence and the Elmwood neighborhood (as did all Broad Street establishments). The impressive interior was the handiwork of architect Arthur Easton. (Above, courtesy of the authors; below, courtesy of the Rhode Island Historical Preservation and Heritage Commission and Warren Jagger.)

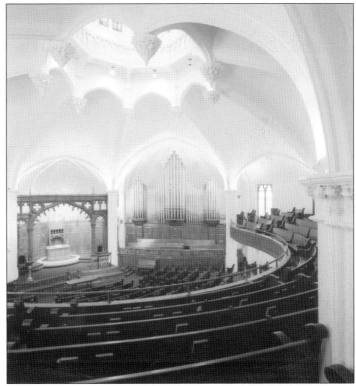

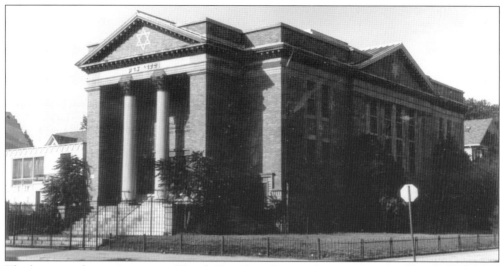

The largest and most imposing of South Providence's several synagogues was Temple Beth El at 688 Broad Street. It housed the Reform Congregation Sons of Israel and David. Built in 1911, it symbolized the prominence already attained by the neighborhood's large Jewish community. When the congregation moved to Orchard Avenue on Providence's East Side in 1954 as part of the neighborhood out-migration that began after World War II, four smaller South Providence Orthodox shuls merged to form Congregation Shaare Zedek and acquired the building. On May 22, 1955, nearly 1,000 Jewish faithful paraded through the streets of South Providence after removing the sacred Torahs from their smaller, obsolete houses of worship. The marchers are shown here as they make their way along Willard Avenue to their new Broad Street home. (Both photographs courtesy of the Rhode Island Jewish Historical Association.)

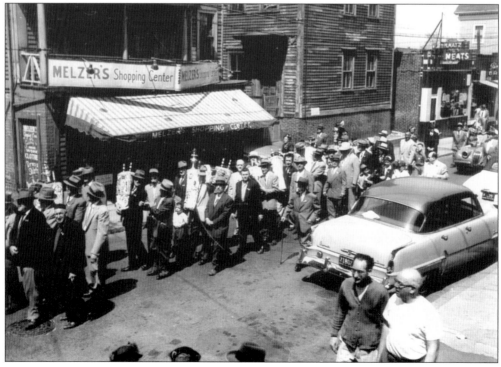

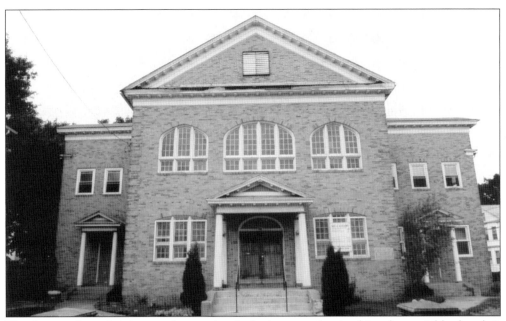

This house of worship is a good example of ethnic succession in this urban neighborhood. It was built on the corner of Prairie Avenue and Potters Avenue in 1888 as St. Paul's Methodist Episcopal Church. Its congregation, formed in 1854, had vacated its church on the corner of Swan and Plain Streets. In 1938, the building was acquired by the Sons of Abraham and remodeled as a synagogue. After the Jewish exodus, it became the Mount Calvary Church of the Deliverance in 1967. Its new tenant was a black congregation that formed as a result of the significant movement of African Americans into South Providence in the 1960s. (Courtesy of the authors.)

The Congregation Beth Israel Anshe Austria held services in this synagogue at 53 Robinson Street until 1954, when the building was demolished as part of an urban redevelopment project. By the time of its demise, the Jewish population of the area was in decline, but most Jewish businesses survived for at least another decade. (Courtesy of the Rhode Island Jewish Historical Association.)

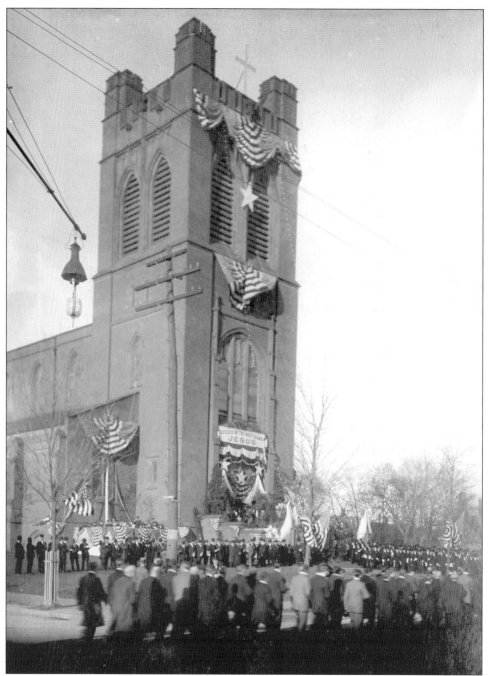

The third and present St. Michael's Church was constructed between 1891 and 1915 in the Anglo-Norman Gothic style of architecture. Its massive tower—40 feet square and rising 156 feet above Oxford Street—dominates the South Providence landscape to this day. More than any other icon, it symbolized the size and the vibrancy of South Providence's Catholic community. In the early 1950s, St. Michael's was reputed to be the largest parish in New England. This unusual photograph depicts a Holy Name Society celebration, with elaborate patriotic decorations, held shortly after the church's completion, perhaps during World War I. (Courtesy of Dr. Thomas Mulvey.)

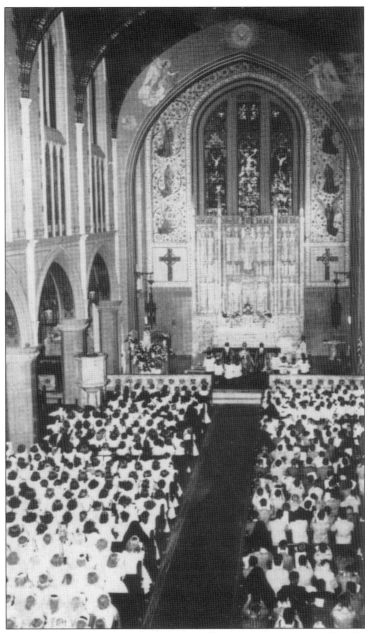

Tens of thousands of parishioners have witnessed the interior splendor of St. Michael's, which was designed (says the 1915 dedication booklet) "to produce a religious atmosphere." The upper church seats more than 1,300 worshipers who gaze upon three altars (executed in Sienna marble quarried at Pietrasanta, Italy) amid 10 massive arches and 20 marble pillars that rise to the vaulted cypress ceiling. In addition to the upper church, the building contains the spacious St. Bernard's Chapel in its basement. Shown here from the choir loft are participants in the annual May procession (around 1955). Not shown is the baptismal font near the church entrance. Fr. Oscar R. Ferland, principal author of St. Michael's centennial booklet, calculated from church records that "as of August 5, 1959, 22,130 children of God" had been baptized there. (Courtesy of the authors.)

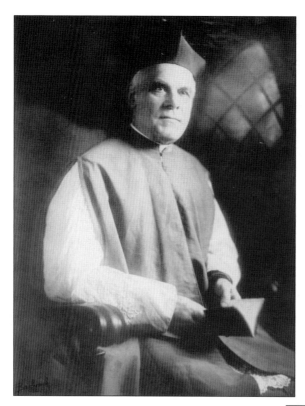

Irish-born monsignor Patrick Farrelly was pastor of St. Michael's Church from May 1912 to December 1935. He had been ordained a priest in 1880 by Bishop Thomas Hendricken (also Irish-born) and apprenticed at Holy Trinity Church in Central Falls before his arrival in South Providence. During his productive tenure, the church was completed (1915), and a rectory (1924), a convent (1929), and the parish school (1925) were built. (Courtesy of the authors.)

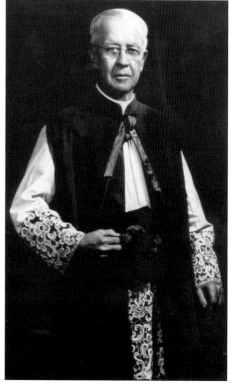

Right Rev. Msgr. Peter E. Blessing, D.D., V.G. (vicar general), was pastor of St. Michael's from 1936 until his death in 1957—the time during which the parish attained its greatest size and influence. A native of South Providence and a graduate of Tyler School and LaSalle Academy, Monsignor Blessing had been pastor of St. Edward's (Wanskuck) and St. Joseph's (Fox Point) and served as rector of the cathedral and editor of the *Providence Visitor* (1909–1913) before assuming the leadership of St. Michael's Parish. Tall, handsome, and courtly, the monsignor was an imposing figure who inspired respect. He served as vicar general—the number-two post in the diocese—under four bishops over a span of four decades (1916–1957). (Courtesy of the authors.)

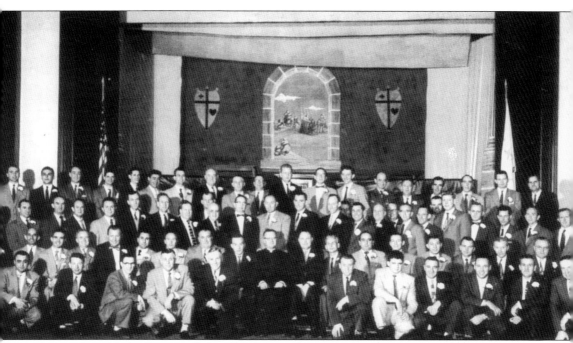

The Knights of Columbus came belatedly to St. Michael's in 1957 despite the fact that Monsignor Blessing had been the order's state chaplain since 1915. Donald Murray, a former state deputy, was chosen first grand knight and a Knights of Columbus hall was opened on Mystic Street. Shown here is the charter class of St. Michael's Council. In the center is the council chaplain, Fr. Oscar R. Ferland. (Courtesy of the authors.)

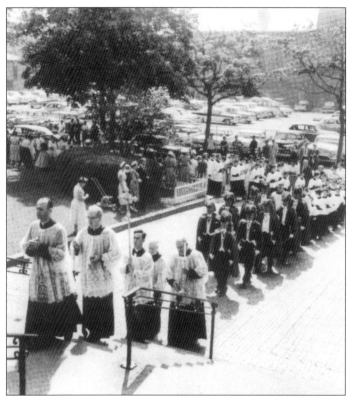

This 1950s procession is typical of the public demonstrations of faith held regularly at St. Michael's Church. Carrying the crucifix (third from left) is the Rev. John Farley, whose father was the caretaker of the church grounds. Farley eventually became the vicar of education for the Diocese of Providence (1973–1983). Behind the priests are fourth-degree members of the Knights of Columbus led by Thomas Conley, grand knight of St. Paul's Council. (Courtesy of the authors.)

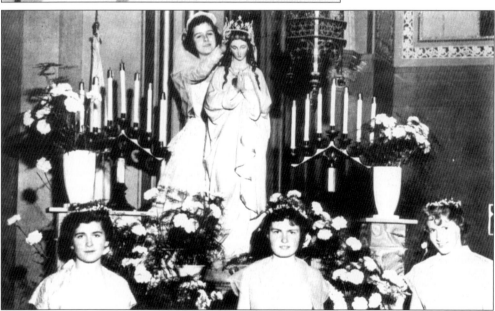

The highlight of St. Michael's annual May procession was the crowning of the Blessed Virgin Mary by members of the Children of Mary Sodality. Doing the honors in this early-1950s photograph are Theresa Ward, placing the crown, assisted by (from left to right) Patricia Loughery, Barbara Windward, and Frances Loughery. The main purpose of the sodality was to foster charity by aiding the poor and needy. (Courtesy of the authors.)

Tyler School third graders Peter and Paul Campbell (right) were recruited by renowned choir director and composer C. Alexander Peloquin in 1956 to perform in the cathedral choir. Long hours of practice culminated in Christmas midnight mass, a pageant-filled tour de force attended by a packed house of more than 2,000 parishioners. During these days, the Campbell twins had little fear in making the half-mile return trek to their tenement on Pearl Street following the lengthy two-and-a-half-hour Christmas service. (Courtesy of the authors.)

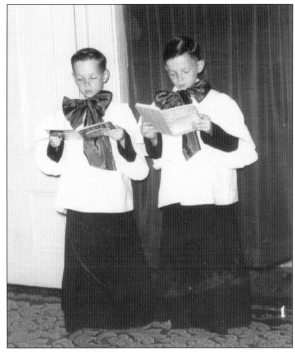

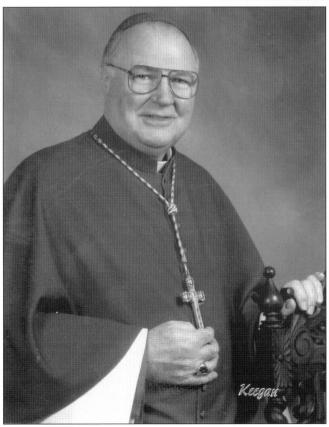

Daniel Patrick Reilly was the sixth oldest of the nine children born to Francis E. Reilly and Mary Reilly (née Burns) of 225–227 Thurbers Avenue. Raised by his widowed mother, Daniel entered the seminary after graduation from St. Michael's School (class of 1943). He was ordained a priest in 1953 and took the fast track to the top: secretary to Bishop Russell McVinney (1956), diocesan chancellor (1964), and vicar general, then bishop of Norwich (1975) and bishop of Worcester (1994). He is the neighborhood's highest ranking cleric. (Courtesy of Daniel Patrick Reilly.)

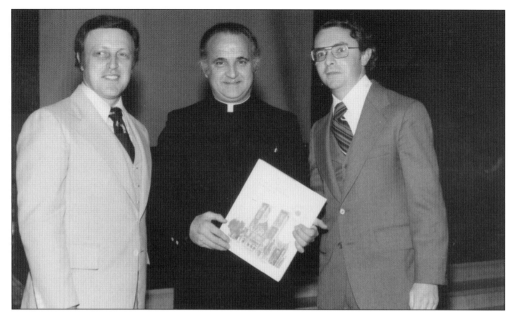

In 1968, Daniel Reilly prevailed upon Patrick Conley (left) and Matt Smith (right) to write a history of the Diocese of Providence for its 1972 centennial observance. Finally, as part of Rhode Island's 1976 bicentennial celebration chaired by Conley, the completed book was presented to Reilly and Fr. Frank Guidice (center), chairman of the Committee on Religion and Social Awareness of the Rhode Island Bicentennial Commission (ri76). The event was held at the cathedral, where Guidice eventually became rector. Matt Smith, a former resident of Ocean Street and the archivist of Providence College, later became speaker of the house and state court administrator. (Courtesy of the authors, photograph by Lou Notarianni.)

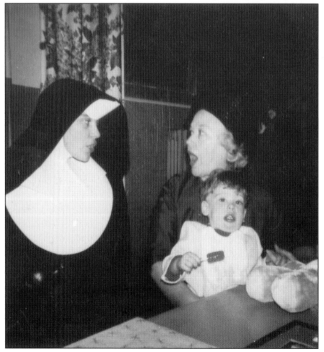

At mid-century and earlier, when a Southside family had one of its members enter religious life, the vocation was a source of pride and satisfaction. So it was for Alice Violet (center) when her bright and feisty daughter Arlene entered the Sisters of Mercy, the order that served both St. Michael's and Cathedral Parishes. The infant in this 1964 family photograph is Alice's grandchild Brad Violet, who became a Providence policeman respected by his peers as "a stand-up guy." (Courtesy of Henry E. "Buddy" Violet.)

Six

SCHOOL DAYS
PAROCHIAL AND PUBLIC

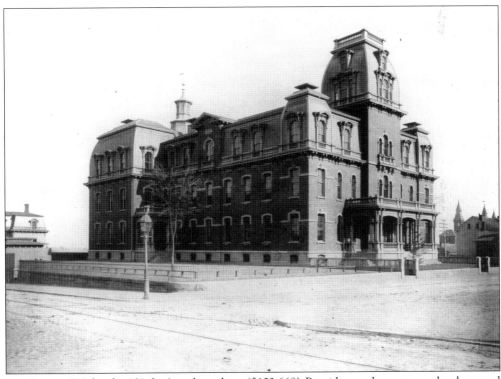

The largest (86 feet by 131 feet) and costliest ($133,668) Providence elementary school erected in the 19th century was the beautifully crafted Point Street Grammar School, built in 1873–1874 in a Second Empire architectural style that anticipated the design of Providence's city hall. At its dedication, it was described as "a palace for the people's children." The building was known for its advanced system of ventilation and its 12-classroom plan, featuring six rooms on each of the first two floors, with assembly rooms and a library under its mansard roof. The splendid Point Street structure (attended by one of the authors) was demolished in 1960 to make way for Route I-95. The only Gilded Age schoolhouse of its type that still survives is South Providence's Beacon Avenue School, rehabilitated as Section Eight housing for the elderly (Courtesy of the authors.)

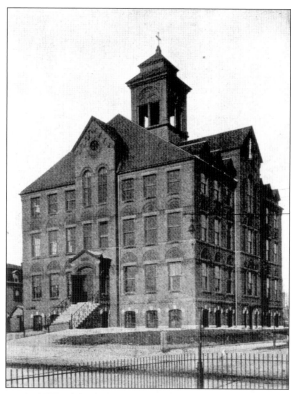

In 1855, Bishop Bernard O'Reilly opened the largest parochial school in the state on Lime Street in his cathedral parish. By 1890, rising enrollments prompted Bishop Matthew Harkins to build a much larger school diagonally opposite the Point Street Grammar School. This facility was named in honor of William Tyler, first bishop of the Diocese of Hartford, who governed his diocese from the Providence cathedral. Tyler School prospered for 70 years until it crossed paths with Interstate 95. A new Tyler School was built at 126 Somerset Street near the South Providence Recreation Center, but it closed in 1973. The Urban Education Center now occupies that site. (Courtesy of the authors.)

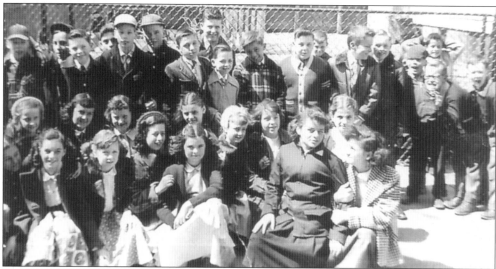

This happy group of fifth-grade pupils at Tyler School poses for the camera in this 1953 photograph. Those whose identities are known are (first row) Margie Rodgers sister of Judge Joe Rodgers (extreme left), Maureen McMullen (third from left), and Mary Turbidy (fourth from left); (second row) Phyllis Marshall (far left) and Katherine Moran, daughter of 11th Ward councilman Pete Moran (seventh from left); (third row) Albert Dumas (far left), Jim Murphy (fifth from left), David Del Padre (sixth from left), George St. Lauren (seventh from left), Frank Darigan (eighth from left), Ray Lomax (ninth from left), Owen McDermott (eleventh from left), Richard Kelly (hands on head), and Tom Louth (extreme right). (Courtesy of Frank Darigan.)

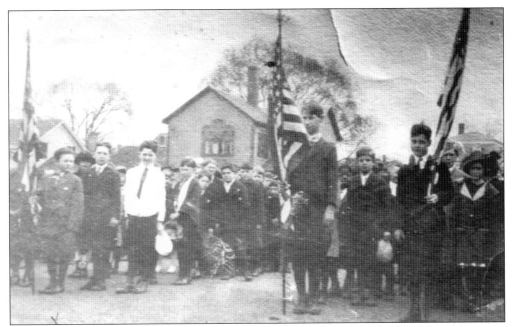

Arbor Day, the second Friday in May, was once a legal holiday in Rhode Island. Its purpose was to encourage the planting of trees to beautify the landscape. This observance was held in 1918 at the Thurbers Avenue School. Thomas Conley (extreme left) built his ice-cream parlor in 1947 on the lot behind him. The school was demolished in 1962 after 90 years of use. Thomas's nephew Bill Conley Jr. acquired the land in 1987 and sold it, in 1992, to the Jehovah's Witnesses, who built a church on the site. (Courtesy of Julia V. Conley.)

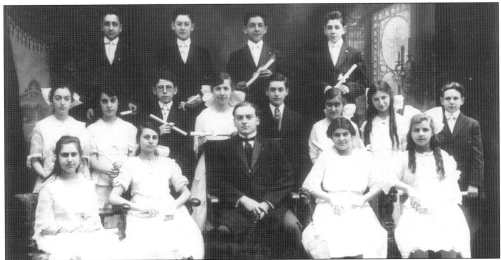

The members of this 1919 confirmation class at Temple Beth-El proudly hold their diplomas. Reform Judaism for a time replaced bar mitzvahs with confirmation for boys and girls. The educational process was conducted at age 16 or 17 because it was deemed a more mature age to assume the obligations of Judaism. These adolescents had been successfully instructed in their communal as well as their religious responsibilities, with their minds prepared for becoming "faithful members of the Jewish congregation, of society, and of the state." (Courtesy of the Rhode Island Jewish Historical Association and Ken Orenstein.)

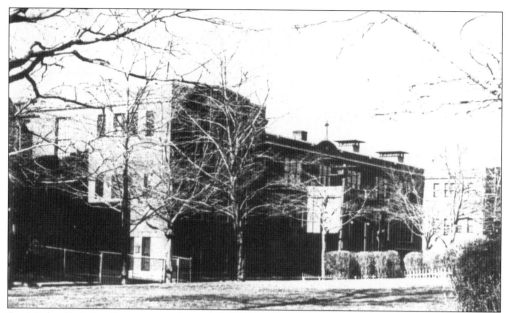

St. Michael's School was opened on Gordon Avenue in September 1925. It began with five grades, but by 1931, it offered instruction for grades one through nine. By 1950, it enrolled over 1,300 pupils and ranked as the largest parochial school in the diocese. The huge out-migration of parishioners forced St. Michael's School to close, but its large, sturdy building was deemed suitable to house the Bishop McVinney Regional School. That institution was established in 1973 to educate students from the four Southside parishes whose schools had been discontinued, namely Cathedral (Tyler), St. Charles, Assumption, and St. Michael's. (Courtesy of the authors.)

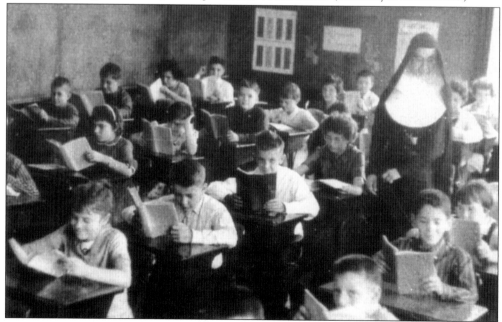

A nun of the Sisters of Mercy keeps a careful eye on her young students. The order taught at Tyler, St. Michael's, St. Aloysuis Orphanage, and St. Xavier Academy, thus exerting a powerful influence on the children of South Providence. (Courtesy of the authors.)

Rose Dorsey of Trask Street, mother of six, chats about their progress with Sr. Marie Rosaire in this early-1950s photograph. Christened Margaret C. Goforth, Sister Rosaire was beloved by her fifth- and sixth-grade students. After leaving St. Michael's, she taught business subjects at several area high schools and was the business department chairman at Bishop Feehan High School in Attleboro at the time of her death in 1986 at the age of 64. (Courtesy of Thomas Dorsey.)

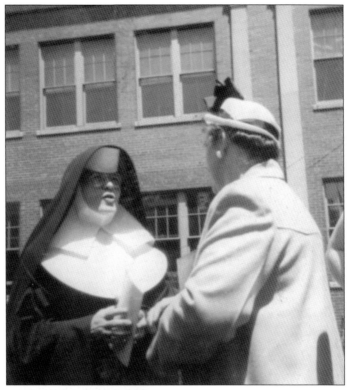

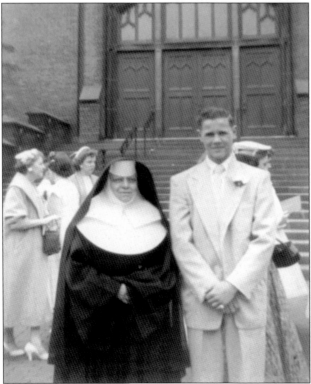

Bill Langlois (class of 1956) of Gladstone Street poses with Sr. Mary Amadeus in front of St. Michael's Church. She was the principal of St. Michael's School from 1931 until the fall of 1958, a period of 27 years. No one had a greater educational impact upon the youth of South Providence than Sister Amadeus. (Courtesy of Bill Langlois.)

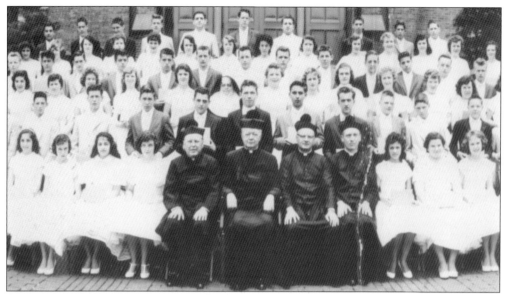

This is a typical picture of a ninth-grade graduation class at St. Michael's School, the sort of picture taken each year. This photograph of the class of 1958 is significant in several respects. It is the last graduation photograph for Sr. Mary Amadeus (third row, sixth from left) and the first for Pastor Cornelius B. Collins, a learned priest who doubled as the chairman of the Rhode Island State Board of Education. The parish priests in the first row are, from left to right, the Reverend Norman LeBoeuf, Father Collins, the Reverend Oscar R. Ferland, and the Reverend Edward W. K. Mullen, who later became a practicing attorney. (Courtesy of Maureen Walsh.)

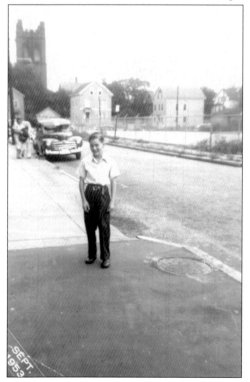

Nine-year-old Bob Walsh of Massie Avenue poses for the camera on the first day of school in 1953. Bob graduated with the St. Michael's class of 1958 (seen above). The massive tower of St. Michael's Church looms in the background. Bob's brother, Joe, who also attended St. Michael's School, later became a prominent attorney, a state senator, mayor of Warwick, and chairman of the board of the Providence Performing Arts Center. (Courtesy of Maureen Walsh.)

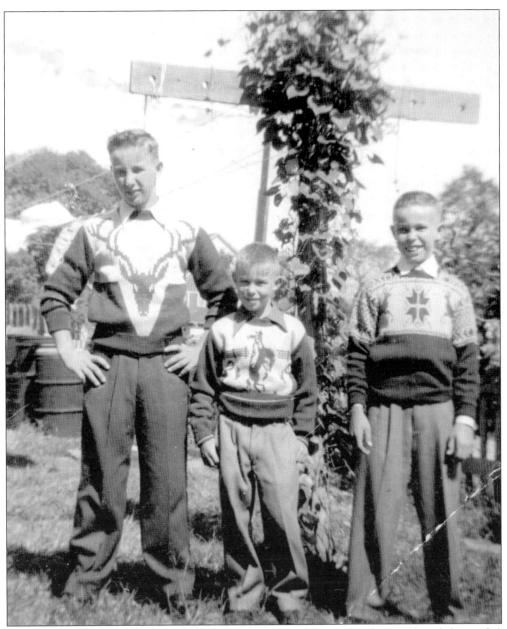

This first-day-of-school photograph dates from 1949. The Johnson brothers—(from left to right) Bob, Ron, and Buddy—are shown at their home at 5 Mutual Street in the so-called Badlands as they head for St. Michael's School. In later life, they became well known for perpetuating both Irish and neighborhood traditions. For many years, they ran the Bowling Green Restaurant on Niantic Avenue, and Harry A. "Buddy" Johnson served as a Southside councilman from 1971 to 1983. Their father, Harry Johnson, became the neighborhood's grand old man, dying in 2005 at the age of 101. (Courtesy of Ron Johnson.)

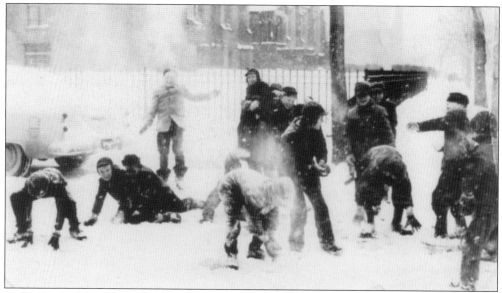

St. Michael's School lacked cafeteria facilities, and most families had only one automobile—the car that was taken to work by dad. Therefore, pupils walked to school in the morning, went home and back for lunch, and walked home again at day's end. Some children lived a mile or more from school because the parish extended west to Elmwood Avenue, south to New York Avenue in Washington Park, and north to Blackstone Street. There were no school buses. Nonetheless, the kids displayed boundless energy, despite the length of the walk or the harshness of the weather. This 1950s free-for-all snowball fight after school exemplifies that hardiness. The rear of the church can be seen in the background. (Courtesy of the authors.)

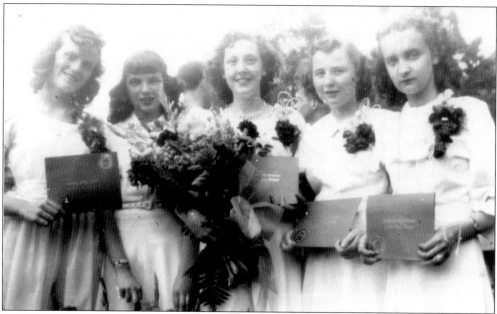

These happy ladies proudly display their diplomas following their graduation from St. Michael's School in 1948. They are, from left to right, Charlotte Johnston, Maureen Carroll, Jane Whitehead, Nancy McWilliams, and June Stone. (Courtesy of Kathy Hinckley.)

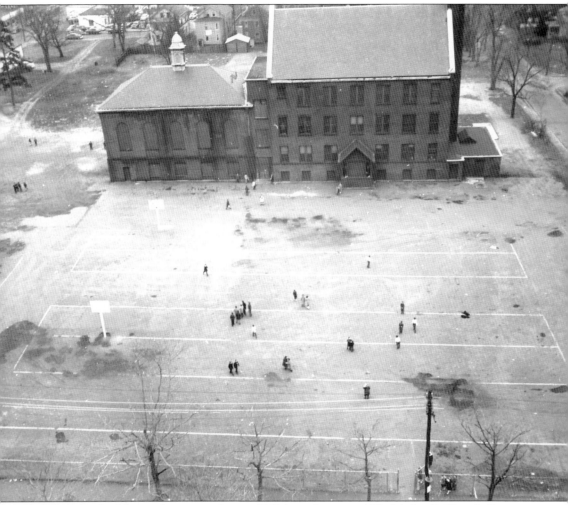

This photograph of the academy was taken in 1959 from the tower of St. Michael's Church. Prior to World War II, the building was used to educate the orphans at adjacent St. Aloysius Home. During the war, it was used by the Coast Guard. Finally it housed grades five and six of St. Michael's School when enrollment peaked in the late 1940s and 1950s. Jim Healey (the elder) conducted a large summer school in the building during the 1960s. After the obsolete structure was demolished, the property was sold in November 1976 to Oxford Place Associates, which built a high-rise apartment house for senior citizens on the site. (Courtesy of the Providence Police Department.)

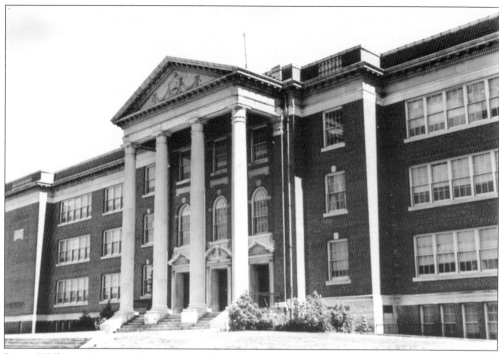

Roger Williams Junior High (now a middle school) was built in 1932. It is a four-story brick and limestone structure in the Georgian Revival style. Its most notable feature (shown here) is its colossal portico. Originally the school had tennis courts to the east, which were surfaced with concrete. Roger Williams was a major educational force on the Southside, drawing students from Washington Park and Elmwood as well as from all of South Providence. Depicted below is the 1944 ninth-grade graduation class. Sam Mulholland, who furnished this photograph, is in the sixth row, second from the left. (Above, courtesy of the Rhode Island Historical Preservation and Heritage Commission; below, courtesy of Sam Mulholland.)

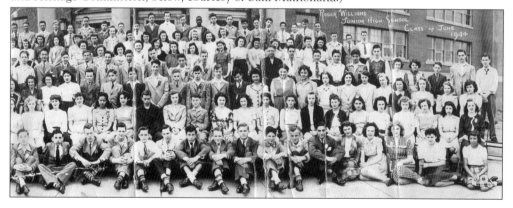

Seven

WORKDAYS
BUSINESS AND LABOR

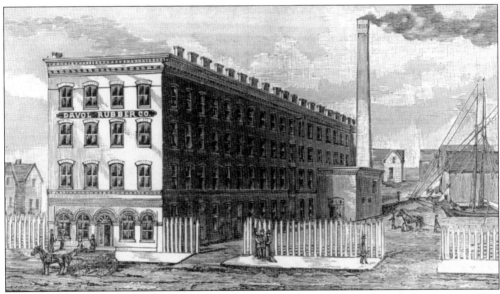

In 1874, Joseph Davol (1837–1909) and Emery Perkins founded Providence's first major rubber manufactory, a firm that assumed the name Davol Rubber Company 10 years after its creation. From a single plant on the south side of Point Street at its intersection with Eddy Street (shown here), Davol expanded to the north side of Point Street from Eddy Street to the bridge, constructing and then enlarging several three- and four-story brick buildings. The company produced an extensive and varied line of items, but it became especially renowned for the fine rubber goods it manufactured for the drug, surgical, dental, and stationery trades, both in this country and worldwide. In 1969, Davol built an additional plant on Sockanosset Crossroads in Cranston as a subsidiary of the International Paper Company, and in 1977, the firm vacated its Point Street buildings for a modern plant in North Carolina. (Courtesy of the authors.)

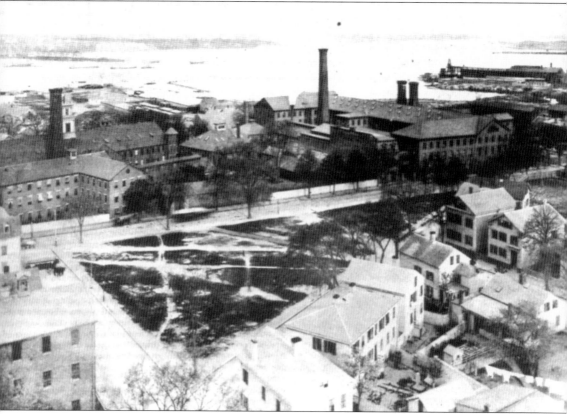

This view of Eddy Street from the Crary Street gasometer dates from 1886. The Providence Machine Company at Franklin Square is on the left, the New England Screw Company is in the center, and the Rhode Island Bleachery is on the right. These large factories provided jobs for the immigrant Irish of Dogtown. All the buildings have been demolished, except for a machine company structure that now houses Desire, a gentleman's club. The Providence Machine Company, founded by Thomas Hill, was the first American firm to manufacture roving machines and fly frames for cotton manufacture. New England Screw was absorbed by the American Screw Company, and its building survived until the recent Interstate 195 relocation project. (Courtesy of the Rhode Island Historical Society.)

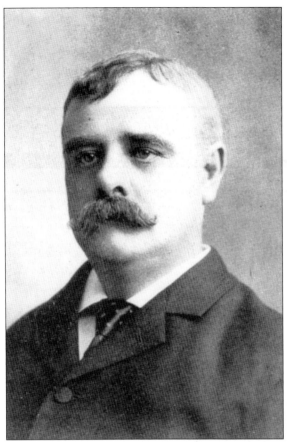

William Henry Luther was Lower South Providence's most prestigious 19th-century citizen. He was the chairman of the board of police commissioners, a commissioner of the fire department, and a prominent manufacturer. His plant at the corner of Oxford and Harriet Streets (still standing) produced high-grade electroplated jewelry, including cuff links, brooches, rings, necklaces, and earrings. By 1890, 26 years after its founding, the company was the largest manufacturer of electroplated jewelry in America. Luther's main building (acquired in 1877) had been known as Temperance Hall when it was constructed by the St. Michael's Abstinence Society. The fire station at 356 Public Street (at the corner of Ocean Street) was known as the William H. Luther Hook and Ladder Company No. 5 because Luther donated its firefighting equipment when it was built in 1885. (Courtesy of the authors.)

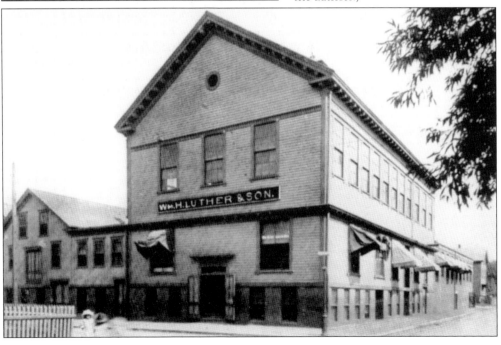

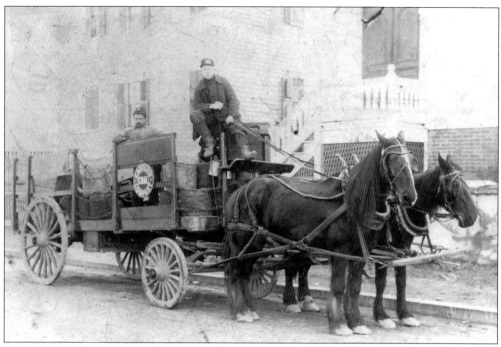

Eastern Coal Company had yards at 184 Dyer Street and at 70 Point Street, where the Narragansett Electric (National Grid) power plant now stands. The company received coal from the colliers that docked at its piers and distributed the fuel via trucks and wagons like this one to homes and businesses. The driver, John A. Powers, belonged to the teamsters union that poses for this photograph in 1910 at Eastern's Point Street facility. Note the union buttons on the teamsters' caps and the presence of black union members. (Both photographs courtesy of the Providence Journal, John Powers, and Scott Molloy.)

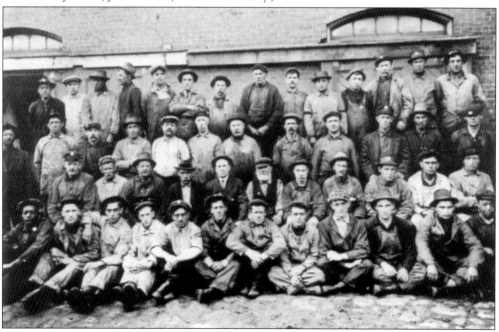

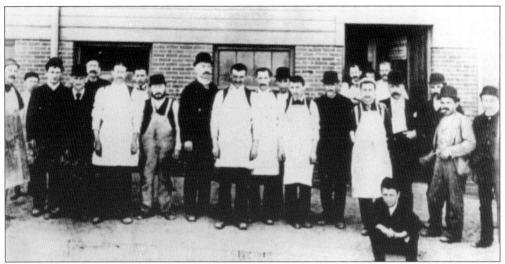

One of the earliest Jewish businesses in the old Dogtown area was the Ludwig-Stern Company, a jewelry manufacturer. It was located on the northwest corner of Blackstone and Gay Streets near the site of the present Edmund W. Flynn Elementary School. From left to right are Simon Horenstein (4th), Samuel Silverman (7th), Abram Jacobs (8th), Simon Goldstein (11th), and Nathan Horovitz (13th). The other men are unidentified. (Courtesy of Isadore S. Horenstein, Esq., and the Providence City Archives.)

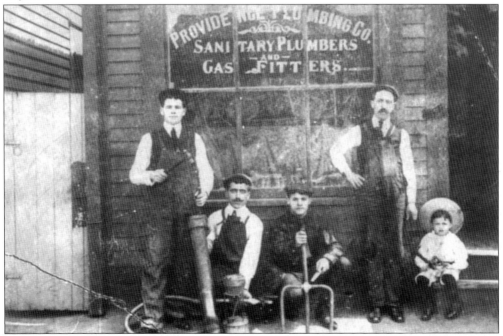

The Providence Plumbing Company operated from this shop at 351 Point Street. Shown in this 1904 photograph, from left to right, are the brothers Abe and Maurice Rotman, an unidentified man, and Frank Scolliard and his son Elisha. Frank soon moved his business to 219 Plain Street and named it Guarantee Plumbing and Heating Company. He built a house next door at 221 Plain Street, which allegedly was the first home in the neighborhood to have electricity. (Courtesy of Ethel Scolliard and the Rhode Island Jewish Historical Association.)

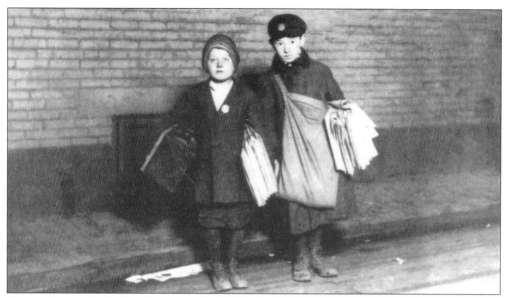

Stanley Steiner (left), bootblack and newsboy, 10 years old, and Jacob Botvin, newsboy, 13 years old, peddle papers in South Providence in this November 1912 photograph taken by Lewis Hine as part of his project to document child labor in Rhode Island. The time of the photograph was one o'clock in the morning. Joseph Jagolinzer, years later, recalled his South Providence experience: "From the time we boys were seven years old we were selling newspapers in downtown Providence . . . As newsboys we had several newspapers to sell—the *Boston American*, the *Providence News*, and the *Providence Journal*. On a big day we could make ten cents." (Courtesy of the Slater Mill Historic Site.)

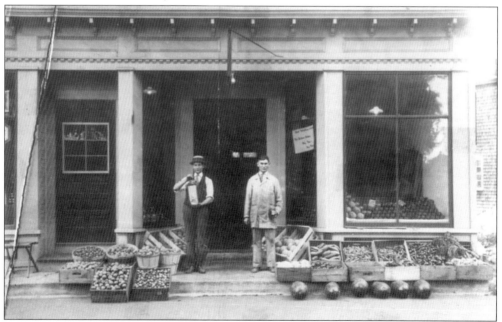

Samuel (left) and David Wiseman pose for the camera in front of their fruit store. The business occupied an enviable spot at the corner of Prairie and Willard Avenues, the crossroads of South Providence's Jewish community. (Courtesy of the Rhode Island Jewish Historical Association.)

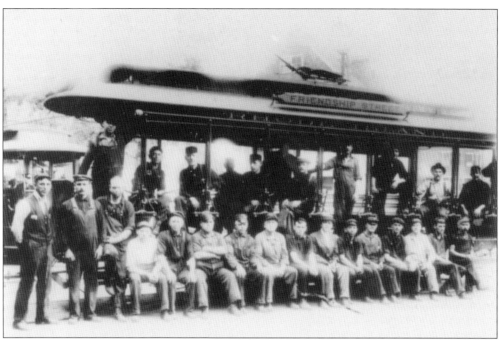

The carmen of the Rhode Island Company (created in 1902 by financier Marsden Perry) were a proud and close-knit labor fraternity. The photograph of the employees of the Friendship Street line (above) and a later view of the South Providence carmen en route to their annual outing give evidence of their solidarity. Labor historian Scott Molloy, who furnished these photographs, has eloquently described the organized carmen's demands for better wages, shorter hours, and safety improvements—and their bond with the riding public—in his 1996 book *Trolley Wars: Streetcar Workers on the Line.* (Courtesy of Scott Molloy.)

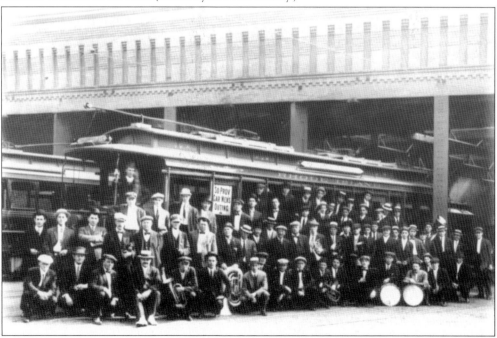

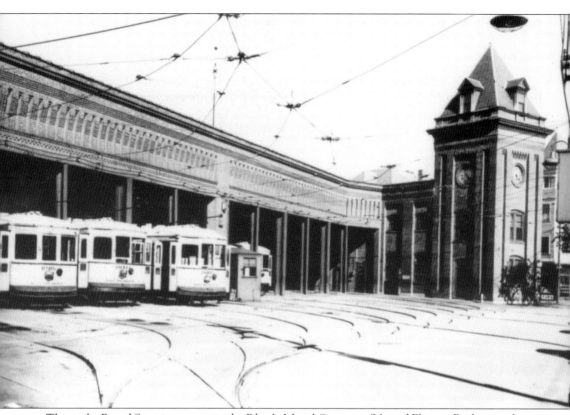

This is the Broad Street entrance to the Rhode Island Company/United Electric Railway carbarn, which occupied a huge parcel bounded southerly by Thurbers Avenue and which extended from Broad Street to Prairie Avenue. This 1900 structure is similar in size and construction to the Union Railroad horsecar barn built here in 1868. The earlier building was replaced when the electrification of the street transit system required a more modern facility. The huge flexible metal overhead doors on the Prairie Avenue side enticed neighborhood boys to hurl their bodies against them to hear the rattle and rumble such contact created. The tower (right) has long since been demolished, but the much-altered building survives. It currently serves as an incubator for several minority businesses, most notably the Omni Development Corporation, a firm that specializes in the creation of affordable housing for today's Southside residents. (Courtesy of Scott Molloy.)

Philip Goldsmith, shown in front of his Prairie Avenue jewelry store, was aptly named. A jeweler, he sold and repaired clocks and watches. Another of his specialties was silver-plated flatware. (Courtesy of the Rhode Island Jewish Historical Association.)

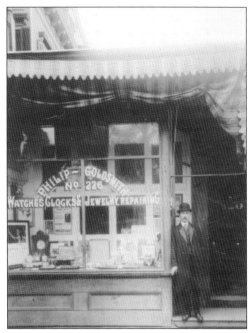

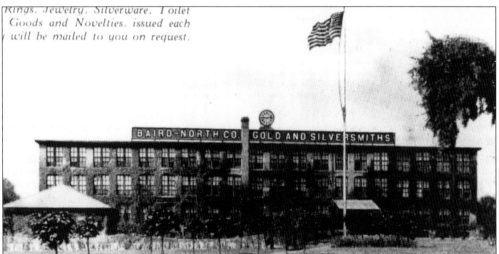

Baird-North Company, a manufacturer and purveyor of gold and silverware, opened this plant at 861 Broad Street in 1907. The building was actually set back to Lexington Avenue with a spacious lawn extending to Broad, upon which a First National Grocery Store was opened in the early 1940s. Baird-North, directed by Alderman George R. Hussey (father of Hollywood actress Ruth Hussey), distributed a wide array of items, including diamonds, fine gold and silver jewelry, rings, watches, leather goods, and tableware. By 1910, the company's advertisements proclaimed that Baird-North was "the world's largest retail mail order jewelers." Its catalog sales slogan was "Direct from the workshop, you saved one-third." During the Great Depression, Baird-North ceased operations at this plant and Hassenfeld Brothers, another jewelry manufacturer, began to operate from the premises. Hassenfeld's tenure extended for a decade, when it was, in turn, succeeded by Cornell-Dublier, an electrical contractor, which was followed by Maurice C. Smith, a shoe manufacturer, who renamed the building the Maurice C. Smith Building and eventually rented portions of it to small businesses. (Courtesy of the authors.)

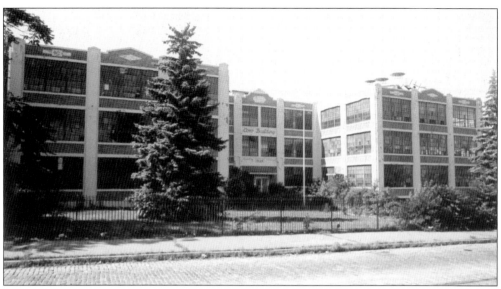

The Coro Company had its origins in New York City, formed a Providence branch in 1911 on Abbott Park Place, and moved to this spacious building at 167 Point Street in 1929. By the 1950s, Coro was reputed to be the country's largest manufacturer of costume jewelry, and it employed many workers from South Providence. After opening several branch plants locally, in 1970 Coro became a subsidiary of Richton International Corporation, which closed its Point Street facility in 1979. Today the building's principal tenant is Lifespan, a hospital consortium. (Courtesy of the Rhode Island Historical Preservation and Heritage Commission.)

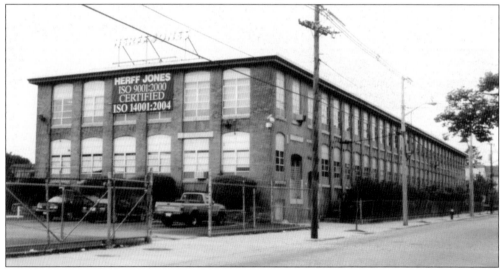

This building at 226 Public Street, near Eddy Street, housed yet another major jewelry manufacturer. Occupied successively from 1910 by Silverman Brothers, Dieges and Clust, and Herff-Jones (the latter an Indiana-based corporation), this plant continues to produce fine jewelry items, including class rings for many secondary schools and colleges and awards for popes, presidents, kings, and athletes. One product is especially noteworthy: this plant crafts the Heisman Trophy, awarded each year to the nation's top collegiate football player. Providence has another connection to the Heisman as well—it was named to honor coach and athletic director John Heisman, who was a student at Brown University from 1887 to 1889. (Courtesy of the authors.)

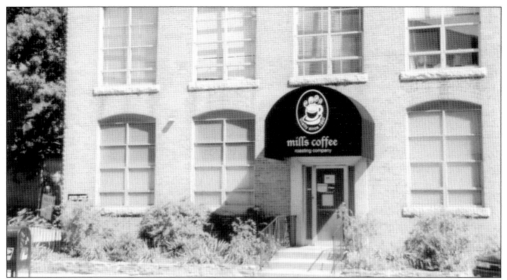

Mills Coffee is a Rhode Island institution, with South Providence connections for three-quarters of a century. Founded by Thomas H. Mills, the company moved to 157 Thurbers Avenue, near Eddy Street, in the early 1930s. After three decades of operation between the Wonder Bar and Conley's Ice Cream Parlor (which served the company's gourmet coffee), Kenny Mills moved his coffee-roasting company to this building at 1058 Broad Street, opposite Sackett Street. (Courtesy of the authors.)

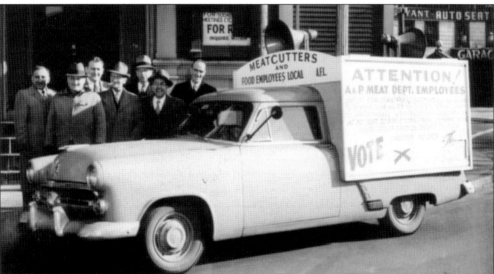

South Providence at mid-century was a working-class, blue-collar neighborhood where union membership was strong. The Carpenter's Local 94 had its hall at the corner of Eddy and Briggs Streets; the Meatcutters and Food Employees Union (shown here) was located on Broad Street near Trinity Square, where the Salvation Army headquarters now stand. Included in this photograph are two future directors of the state department of labor, Sam DiSano and Romeo Calderone. The Meatcutters' Hall was often rented by neighborhood residents for social events. Both unions have long since vacated the neighborhood, the carpenters moving to Jefferson Boulevard in Warwick and the food and commercial workers to Silver Spring Street in the North End. (Courtesy of Scott Molloy.)

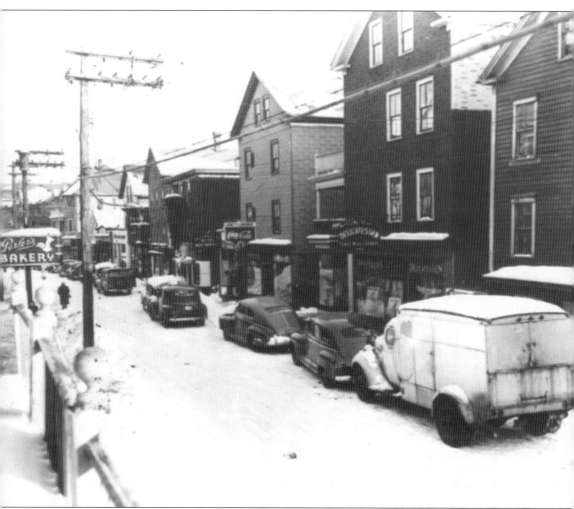

Willard Avenue was the center of the Jewish district and South Providence's main commercial entrepot. Eleanor F. Horvitz, the area's most knowledgeable historian, describes this scene as follows: "Williard Avenue, looking east, circa 1947. Appearing in the photo are Perler's Bakery on the left (No. 207) and on the opposite side of the street from right to left Louis Bezviner, grocer (No. 214); N.Y. Delicatessen and Public Model Creamery (No. 208); Jewett's Creamery (No. 204); Bazarsky's Meat Market (No. 202); Snell's Bakery (No. 200); Harry's Fruit Market (No. 196); Spiegel's Meat and Poultry (No. 190); Keller's Meat Market (No. 184½); and Samuel Bernstein Meats (No. 182)." (Courtesy of the Providence City Archives.)

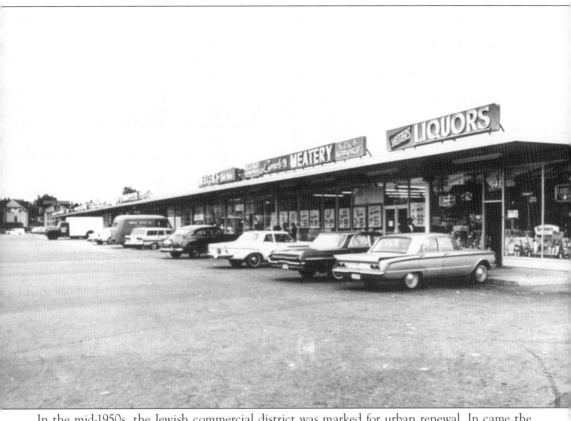

In the mid-1950s, the Jewish commercial district was marked for urban renewal. In came the bulldozers for a vain attempt to reshape the neighborhood in the image of suburbia. In 1956, the Willard Shopping Center (shown here) was built on the easterly side of Prairie Avenue just south of Willard Avenue. The project was short-lived. By the end of the 1960s, it had succumbed to vandals and to the destructive racial rioting that marked that decade. Several social service agencies now occupy newer buildings on the site. (Courtesy of the Providence City Archives.)

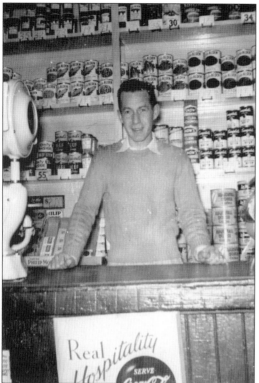

For many years, Roland Campbell operated Campbell's Market, a small variety store on Pine Street adjacent to the historic William H. Dyer House (1842). Stores like this dotted the streets of South Providence, supplying residents with their basic everyday needs and creating a stable and personal world for customers and merchants alike. (Courtesy of the authors.)

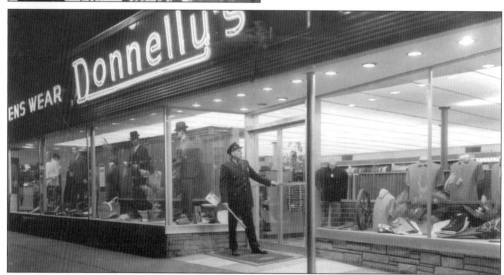

Donnelly's Men's Wear had been a neighborhood fixture since 1940. Its building at 790 Broad Street had been an A&P supermarket until that operation moved south on Broad to a new store between Byfield and Aldrich Streets. Donnelly's was easily the most stylish clothing outlet in South Providence. It also specialized in the sale of school uniforms, mainly to students in Catholic schools. Before this landmark closed in 1999, Donnelly's had established stores in seven other Rhode Island communities. Competition from the malls changed all that. Today Donnelly's School Apparel at 333 Niantic Avenue is the only survivor, and the original Broad Street store is now occupied by the Tides School. (Courtesy of the Providence Police Department.)

Eight

PLAY DAYS
SPORTS

Andy Coakley's (1882–1963) first encounter with baseball was on a field where St. Michael's Church is now located. His mentor was Tim O'Neil. Coakley pitched in the major leagues from 1902 through 1911 for the Philadelphia Athletics of Connie Mack and then briefly for the Cincinnati Reds, Chicago Cubs, and New York Yankees. His peak year was 1905, when he compiled a record of 20-7 and registered a league-leading winning percentage of .741 while guiding the A's to the American League pennant. Coakley is best remembered as the man who mentored Lou Gehrig at Columbia University, where he coached baseball from 1915 to 1951. Columbia's baseball field is dedicated in Coakley's honor. (Courtesy of the authors.)

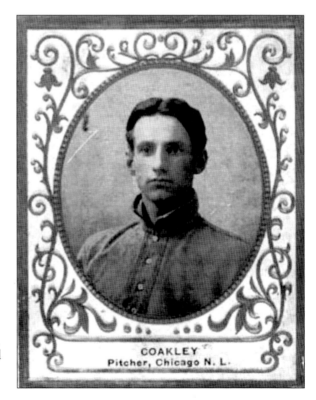

COAKLEY
Pitcher, Chicago N. L.

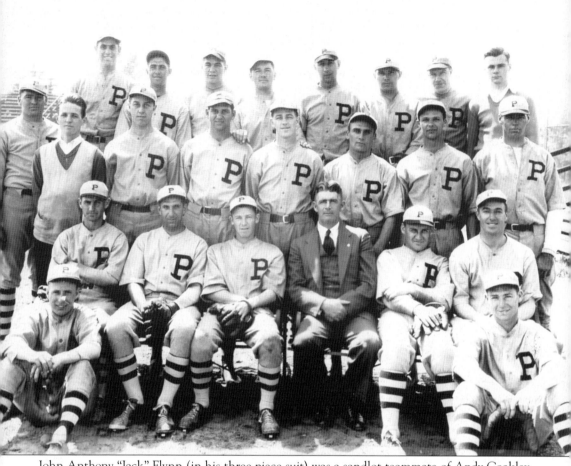

John Anthony "Jack" Flynn (in his three-piece suit) was a sandlot teammate of Andy Coakley. He played three seasons of major-league ball, from 1910 through 1912, as first baseman with the Pittsburgh Pirates and the Washington Senators. His career batting average was a modest .249, but as coach of the Providence College baseball team, he chalked up a far more impressive average. During his 10 seasons as Providence College mentor (1924, 1925, and 1927 to 1934, a stint interrupted in 1926 by a year as coach of New Haven in the Class A Eastern League), he compiled a winning percentage of .725—a mark no subsequent coach has equaled. Under Flynn's guidance, Providence College won three Eastern Regional baseball championships—1928, 1931, and 1932—with Flynn compiling a coaching record of 147-55-2 against collegiate competition. On May 24, 1932, Flynn's Friars (shown here) won their most notable victory when the Boston Red Sox came to Providence. Aided by Red Sox errors, Providence College rallied for five runs in the last of the ninth inning and a 9-8 victory—the kind of amazing comeback of which legends are made. (Courtesy of the Providence College Archives.)

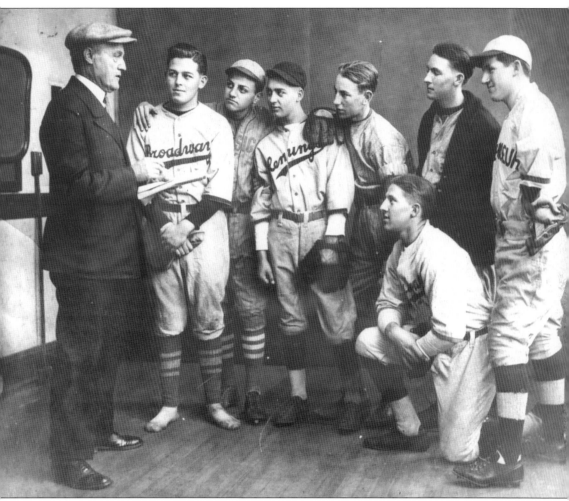

With professional sports nearly dormant on the local level during the Depression, sandlot baseball reached the peak of its popularity. By that time, Providence had developed one of the largest and best-run sandlot systems in the nation. The credit for such a comprehensive program goes to Dogtown's Tim O'Neil, "King of the Sandlots." On Saturdays from early May through Labor Day, a total of seven leagues (based on age), each with eight teams (usually recruited from the neighborhoods), competed on the ball fields of Metropolitan Providence. Figuring on the basis of 21-game schedule, nearly 600 contests were played each season, with the best teams drawing more than 1,000 spectators per game. O'Neil, who began his baseball career as a coach in the 1890s, directed the teams of St. Michael's Parish, which boasted such young stars as future major-leaguers Andy Coakley and Jack Flynn. In 1902, he began the system eventually called the Tim O'Neil Leagues, for which he became nationally recognized. O'Neil is shown in this 1930 photograph with some of his boys. Immediately next to O'Neil is Warren Walden, who became a well-known sports commentator and pioneer television newsman and who later assumed the awesome task of directing the league. To Walden's left is John A. Notte Jr., who served as governor of the state from 1959 to 1961. The ball field at Roger Williams Park was dedicated to O'Neil in 1946 several months before the death of the man who always maintained that "there is no such thing as a bad boy." (Courtesy of Warren Walden.)

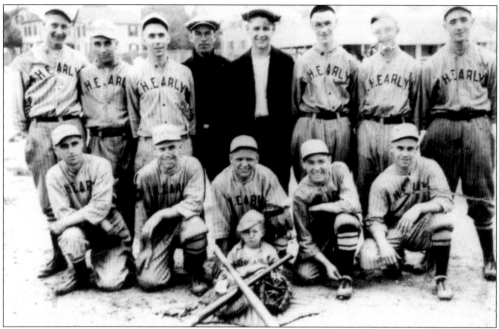

T. H. Early was the neighborhood's top sandlot baseball team in the sports-crazed decade of the 1920s. The company, which specialized in machinery and furniture moving, was located at 283 Thurbers Avenue, and its founder, Thomas H. Early, lived next door. Most of the players in this 1924 Richardson Park photograph are unidentifiable except for James F. Jackson (first row, third from left) and third baseman Patrick J. "Packy" McKiernan (second row, second from left). (Courtesy of Helen Jackson Petterson and Don McKiernan.)

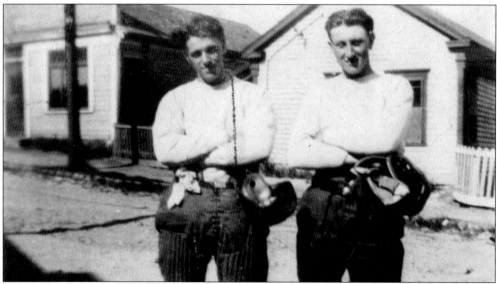

Sandlot football, although much less popular than baseball, had its adherents, like these two robust linemen for the South Providence Argonauts. Depicted in this late-1920s photograph are Joe Bernardi (left) and Bill Conley. The Argonauts' claim to fame was a standoff scrimmage with the great Brown University "Iron Men" of 1926, a football team that compiled a record of 9-0-1 and tied Navy for the championship of the East. (Courtesy of Julia Maney Conley.)

John Aloysius McIntyre of 484 Prairie Avenue became the neighborhood's football hero in 1939, when he was the starting center for the University of Notre Dame and a participant in the annual North-South All-Star Game. In the years after graduation, he became an even greater hero as a navy combat pilot. McIntyre was a flying ace, serving in World War II and Korea. When he retired as a commander, his decorations included the Silver Star, two Distinguished Flying Crosses, and four Air Medals. His first cousins and neighbors John O'Rourke and John Moran (of Budweiser fame) were also gifted athletes. O'Rourke captained the baseball and football teams at Georgetown University; Moran captained baseball and starred in football at Manhattan College. (Courtesy of the Notre Dame Sports Information Department.)

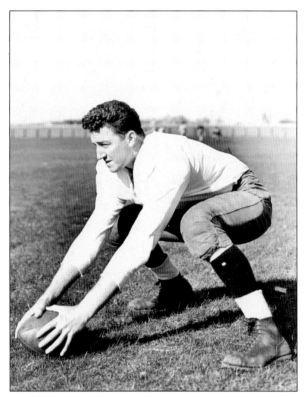

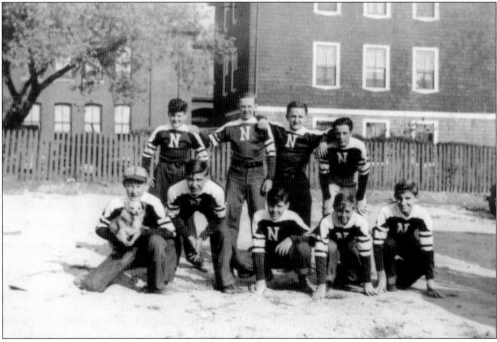

This *Providence Journal* newsboy touch football team from South Providence was no match for the Argonauts or Notre Dame, but it produced at least one stellar performer—Bishop Daniel Patrick Reilly (first row, center). (Courtesy of Bishop Daniel Patrick Reilly.)

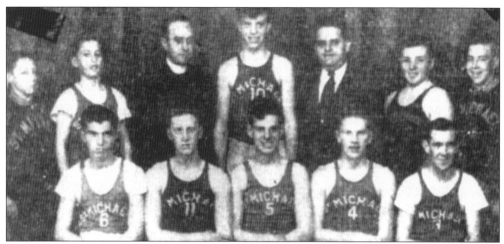

St. Michael's School was not as well regarded for basketball as it was for baseball. Nonetheless, it produced several Catholic Youth Organization championship teams from the 1940s onward, including this 1943 junior high school squad. Pictured from left to right are (first row) Walter "Hago" Harrington, Don Gumbley, James "Lou" Gorman, Al Shields, and Ray Corcoran; (second row) two unidentified players, the Rev. Henry Shelley (the team coach and moderator), John McCauley, Mike Cardillo (Catholic Youth Organization director for the diocese), Jimmy Anderson, and Josie McGovern. (Courtesy of James "Lou" Gorman.)

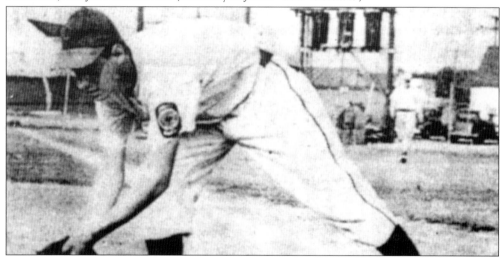

First baseman James Gorman of Briggs Street adopted the nickname "Lou" in emulation of his idol, Lou Gehrig. His other idol was his father, Leo Gorman, a fire department battalion chief who led Providence to national prominence in the field of fire prevention in the 1950s. Lou starred in baseball and basketball on the sandlot, at LaSalle Academy, and at Stonehill College, where he is a legend. After a distinguished career in the U.S. Navy, Lou entered professional baseball, not as a player but as an executive. He helped build two expansion clubs, the Kansas City Royals and the Seattle Mariners, as well as the New York Mets before finally getting the opportunity in 1984 to direct his favorite team, the Boston Red Sox. For 10 tumultuous years, he constructed Red Sox teams that came close but could never quite win the World Series. Lou continues to live near Boston and work for the Red Sox in a public relations capacity. He recently published a memoir—*One Pitch from Glory*—about his decade of directing the Red Sox. (Courtesy of James "Lou" Gorman.)

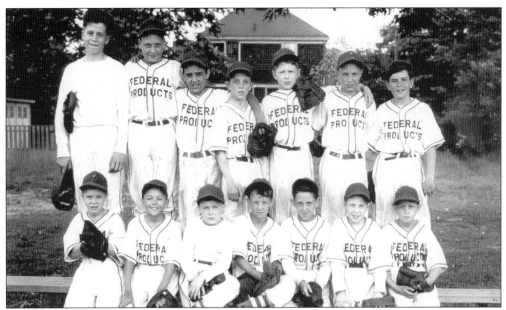

The South Providence–Elmwood Little League was the first league of its kind in Rhode Island. It was formed in 1951 with four original teams: Monowatt Electric, Lovett Beef, Dunne Ford, and Federal Products. All games were played at either the Monowatt field, located off Elmwood Avenue where Hamlin and Dixon Streets dead end, or at the Providence Gas Company field on Allens Avenue, just south of Harbor Junction. Neither field exists today. This photograph, taken at the Monowatt field, shows the original Federal Products team. Pictured are, from left to right, (first row) Jackie Callaghan, Alan Reilly, Jackie Nottage, Ken Mahoney, Jackie Apice, Paul Donahue, and Billy Krans; (second row) Rod Durell, Arthur Krans, Ray Burns, Billy Conley, Vinnie Donahue, Vinnie Ciceri, and Paul McHale. The coaches (not in the picture) were Bob Finch and Frank Shea. (Courtesy of Jack Apice.)

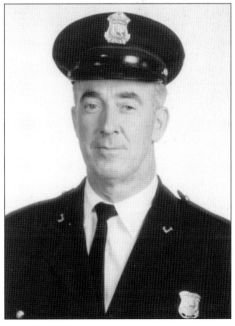

In South Providence, the cop on the beat was more a friend and a mentor to neighborhood kids than a feared enforcer. This rapport existed in large measure because of the Junior Police Athletic Program, and no one better exemplified the role of policeman as peacemaker than officer John Flynn. He was a 43-year-old, 17-year veteran on the force when he assembled the South Providence Junior Police squad that became the nucleus for the great Richardson Park baseball teams of the mid-1950s. Flynn's 14-year-old recruits, coached by Joe Pina, compiled a 6-0 record en route to the 1953 Providence Community League title. (Courtesy of the Providence Police Department.)

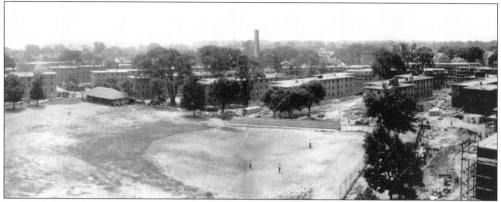

Richardson Park was established as a playground in 1906, and it acquired two additional acres by 1930. During the Depression decade, the federal Works Progress Administration built large concrete grandstands and other amenities, so when this 1942 photograph was taken during the construction of Roger Williams Homes, Richardson Park had become South Providence's premier and only full-sized ballpark. This decade did not produce any home teams to rival the T. H. Early squad of the 1920s or the Independent British-American Association champions of the 1950s, but it produced several ballplayers of great ability, including James "Lou" Gorman, Don Gumbley, John McCauley, Josie and Fran McGovern, Frank and Joe Little, Fr. John Gray, Joe Gray, Walter "Hago" Harrington, and a trio of All-State high school pitchers—Jimmy Anderson (LaSalle), Bob Newton (Hope), and Tommy Paige (Central). The playground's director was Tom McElroy, former Providence College pitching star. (Courtesy of the Rhode Island Historical Society.)

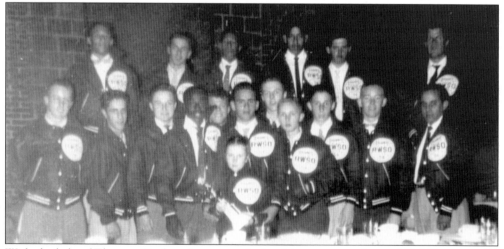

With the help of Thomas Conley, the owner of a local ice-cream parlor, and Ted Sherman, the head of the Roger Williams Homes Tenant Association, officer John Flynn's Junior Police squad evolved into the Roger Williams Social Organization team and entered the Tim O'Neil Leagues in 1954. By season's end, Roger Williams Social Organization had compiled an 18-4 record and won the Circuit League (16 and under) crown. In this photograph, taken after a victory banquet at the project's administration building, team members display their championship jackets. From left to right are (first row): Patrick Conley, Dom Petrarca, Gene McKenna, coach Joe Pina, Virgil Hepler, captain Frank "Peanuts" Viera, Jim McCormick, Jimmy Ballou, Dick Lyons, Artie Anderson, and assistant coach Nick Villella; (second row) Jimmy Potter, Guy Susi, Glen Mabray, Ronald "Champ" Guy, Jack "Cappy" Butler, and Al Roberts. The team mascot, holding the trophy, is Rosemary Conley. (Courtesy of Jim Ballou.)

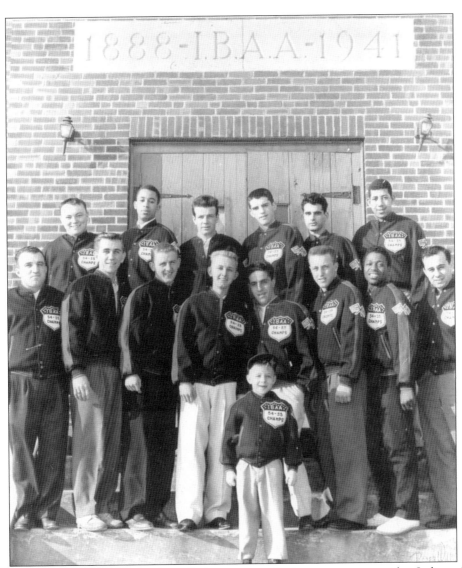

In 1955 and 1956, the Richardson Park team acquired a new sponsor, the Independent British-American Association, but there was no change in its winning ways. The 1955 team (shown here) won the Tim O'Neil Leagues title for 18 year olds with a record of 18-2; the 1956 team compiled a 19-1 record, capturing the Independent Amateur League crown for players 21 and younger. Pictured are, from left to right, (first row) Pete Rousseau (Independent British-American Association president), Paul Vellucci, Ed Ferns, Jim Ballou, Dom Petrarca, Patrick Conley, Joe Pina, and coach Nick Villella; (second row) Dan Rice, Glen Mabray, Hal Quirk, George Brown, Don Annarino, and Champ Guy. Nicky Villella (front) was the team's mascot. Conspicuously missing from the photograph were the squad's superstar—Jack Jordan—a versatile athlete who was the All-State pitcher in baseball and All-American quarterback in football in 1956 while starring for St. Raphael Academy; catcher Jim Healey, the team's leading hitter, who made All-State at LaSalle Academy both in the 300-yard dash and as an outfielder; All-State third baseman Pete Vitullo; and ace right-handed pitcher Al Roberts, who was LaSalle's baseball cocaptain in 1955, an honor he shared with his Independent British-American Association teammate George Brown. (Courtesy of the authors.)

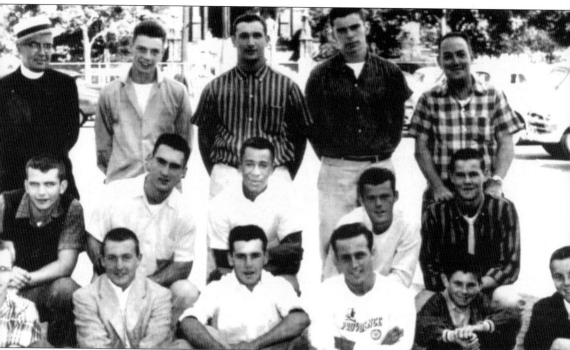

The fifth and final championship for the Richardson Park team was the 1957 state Catholic Youth Organization (CYO) crown. Playing for St. Michael's, this group compiled a record of 10-3 (with one loss by forfeit and another by upset in the New England CYO championship game). This photograph was taken in the academy school yard with St. Michael's Church in the background. From left to right are (first row) cocaptain Jim Ballou, Ed Little, Thomas Dorsey, cocaptain Patrick Conley, and batboys Stu Crowley and Ed Greenan; (second row) Don Foley, Jim Healey, Glen Mabray, Virgil Hepler, and Bill Langlois; (third row) longtime coordinator of St. Michael's youth activities Fr. Henry Shelly, Pat Hurley, Pete Vitullo, Bob McCauley, and coach Jim Healey, who earned Catholic Youth Organization Man of the Year honors for his work with the youth of St. Michael's Parish and who later became a deacon. (Courtesy of the authors.)

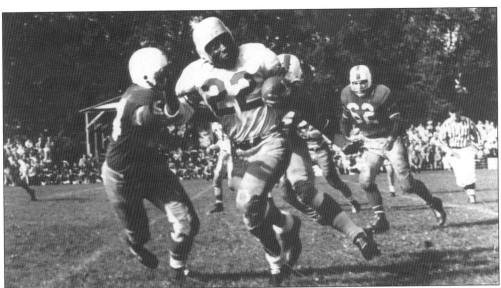

Bernie Pina is en route to a LaSalle Academy touchdown and All-State honors in this 1950 photograph. During the early 1950s, Bernie ("Little Slick") and his younger brothers Tommy and "Handsome Joe" of 127 Rugby Street constituted South Providence's preeminent athletic family. Bernie, who became a highly respected high school coach, twice earned All-State honors in football at LaSalle, where he starred in basketball and track as well. He also excelled in these sports at the University of Rhode Island, earning All-Yankee Conference honors as a halfback in the great Ram backfield that included future professional star Pat Abbruzzi. Tommy followed his older brother as a two-time All-State halfback at LaSalle. Joe, who did not attend high school or college, compiled a remarkable record as an amateur and semiprofessional athlete in baseball, football, slow-pitch softball, and track. He is widely regarded as Rhode Island's fastest sprinter of all time. Though Joe lacked formal training and ran on substandard surfaces, he repeatedly ran under 10 seconds in the 100-yard dash, and once recorded a time of 9.6 seconds in that event. (Courtesy of Bernie Pina.)

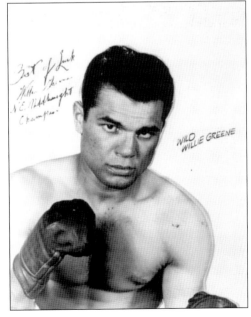

Willie Greene was another versatile South Providence athlete. He excelled in track, football, and boxing. No neighborhood fighter ever achieved such prominence. "Wild Willie," as he was affectionately called, became the New England middleweight champion and the seventh-ranked middleweight in the world in the days when there was one division and one official ranking. After his competitive days were over, Greene became the chief sparring partner for Boston's Paul Pender, the world middleweight champion. An ethnic combination of Irish and Native American, Greene has assumed the name Eagle Heart and the leadership of the Seaconke tribe of the Wampanoag Nation in his tribe's quest for federal recognition. (Courtesy of Germaine Greene.)

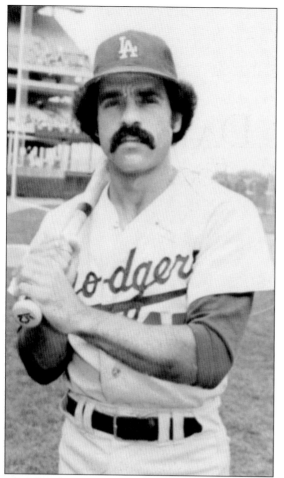

Davey Lopes has emerged as South Providence's most prominent and successful professional athlete. Born in East Providence and raised in Fox Point and South Providence, Lopes began his extraordinary career in the Fox Point Little League and then became an All-State baseball and basketball player at LaSalle Academy (class of 1963). He went on to star with the Los Angeles Dodgers and then played with the Oakland A's, the Chicago Cubs, and the Houston Astros. Lopes batted .308 in four World Series, played in four straight All-Star Games, and won a Golden Glove Award. He twice led the National League in stolen bases (77 was his seasonal high) and once held the major-league record for most consecutive successful steals (38). Since his retirement as an active player in 1987, Lopes has been a coach or manager with several major-league teams. The South Providence Recreation Center on Dudley Street, where Lopes played as a youth, has been named in his honor. During the 1950s, this facility, which contained a full-size basketball court inside and a large outdoor swimming pool, operated under the capable direction of Joe DeStefano and Joe Feeney. (Courtesy of the authors.)

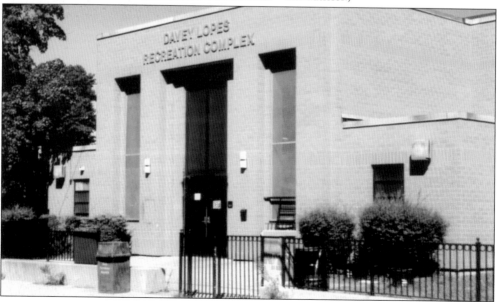

Nine

PLAY DAYS
FUN AND FOOD

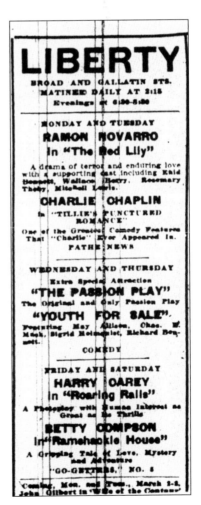

LIBERTY

BROAD AND GALLATIN STS.
MATINEE DAILY AT 2:15
Evenings at 6:30-8:30

MONDAY AND TUESDAY
RAMON NOVARRO
In "The Red Lily"

A drama of terror and enduring love
with a supporting cast including Enid
Bennett, Wallace Beery, Rosemary
Theby, Mitchell Lewis.

CHARLIE CHAPLIN
In "TILLIE'S PUNCTURED
ROMANCE"
One of the Greatest Comedy Features
That "Charlie" Ever Appeared In.
PATHE NEWS

WEDNESDAY AND THURSDAY
Extra Special Attraction
"THE PASSION PLAY"
The Original and Only Passion Play

"YOUTH FOR SALE"
Featuring May Allison, Chas. W.
Mack, Sigrid Holmquist, Richard Ben-
nett.

COMEDY

FRIDAY AND SATURDAY
HARRY CAREY
In "Roaring Rails"

A Photoplay with Human Interest as
Great as the Thrills

BETTY COMPSON
In "Ramshackle House"

A Gripping Tale of Love, Mystery
and Adventure

"GO-GETTERS," NO. 5

Coming Mon. and Tues., March 2-3,
John Gilbert in "Wife of the Centaur"

The Liberty Theater opened in 1921 at 1017 Broad Street. It soon became the most popular entertainment venue on the city's south side. This typical neighborhood theater was part of a chain of movie houses built by Samuel Bomes. During the 1920s, silent films were shown like those listed in this advertisement. During the 1940s and 1950s, westerns were the rage, and the Saturday matinees were packed with screaming children who paid 12¢ to see cartoons and their favorite cowboy. The Liberty closed in the 1960s, then reopened briefly and unsuccessfully as the Art Cinema before becoming a warehouse for used furniture and other items. Plans are currently under way to restore the building as the Liberty Theater Cultural Center, a facility for arts and education. (Courtesy of the authors.)

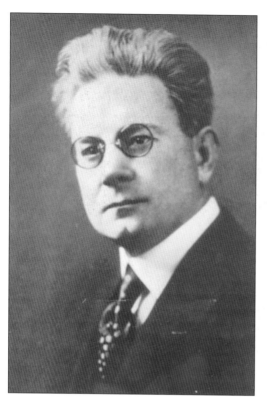

Edward M. Fay, a Dogtown native, was Rhode Island's entertainment impresario during the early decades of the 20th century. He began his varied career as a violin soloist, operated dancing pavilions at Rhodes on the Pawtuxet in Cranston, and Hunt's Mills in East Providence, directed his own orchestra as well as David W. Reeves's American Band, and helped to introduce vaudeville to Providence. In 1916, Fay turned to theater management, acquiring the former Union Theater on downtown Union Street and converting it to Fay's Theater. Thereafter he acquired theaters in New York City, Rochester, and Philadelphia, as well as five additional Providence movie houses: the Emery (Carlton), Majestic, Rialto, Modern, and Capitol. (Courtesy of the authors.)

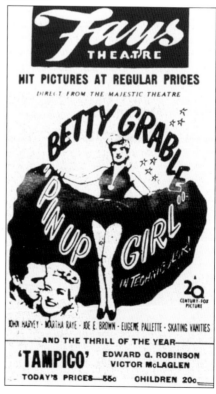

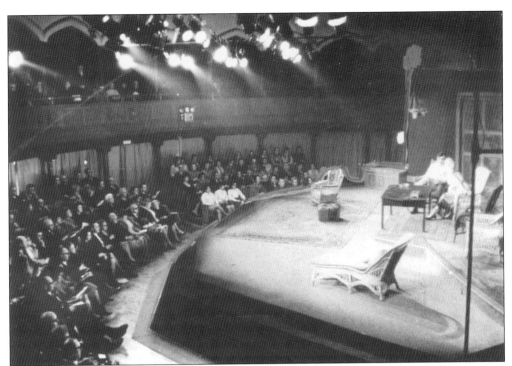

On March 14, 1964, nationally renowned Trinity Repertory Theater debuted in the basement of Trinity Methodist Church on Broad Street. Although it was born on the Southside, its founders and sponsors, led by attorney Milton Stanzler, Norman Tilles, Barbara Orson, Robert and Susan Kaplan, and Roz Goldberg, were mainly from Providence's East Side. Originally styled Trinity Square Playhouse, the group acquired and renovated a theater that had been established by the Reverend Richard Waters, the assistant minister at Trinity Church, to stage some of his own religious plays. Shown here are the original theater (above) and the cast of Brendan Behan's *The Hostage*, the first play staged by the new repertory theater group. (Courtesy of Milton Stanzler.)

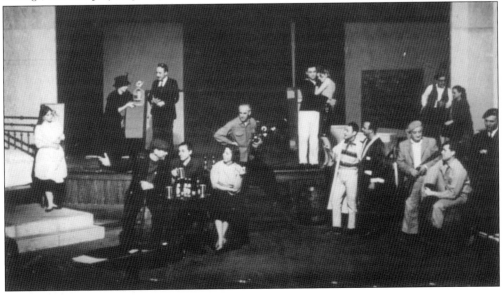

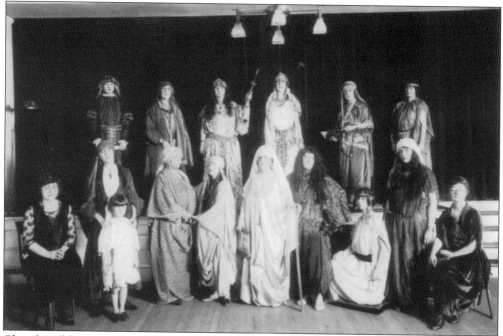

Churches (like Trinity) and synagogues often used plays and dramatic presentations, both to entertain and to instruct. An elaborate example of this approach is the pageant, Women of the Bible, staged here by the children of Temple Beth El. (Courtesy of the Rhode Island Jewish Historical Association.)

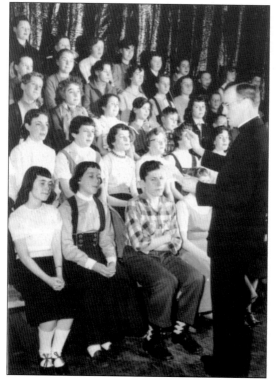

The annual minstrels at Tyler School were designed more to inspire fun than faith. In this 1956 photograph, Fr. Corneluis Lynch gives direction to the cast. Listening intently are a tight-lipped Arlene Violet (first row, second from left) and her schoolmate Frank Darigan (first row, third from left). (Courtesy of Frank Darigan.)

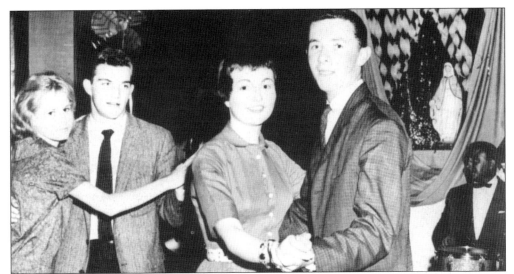

In September 1957, St. Michael's formed a Catholic Youth Organization council, and Jim Sullivan was elected its first president. He was succeeded by Matt Smith, who, in turn, was followed by Ray LaBelle. The most popular youth council functions were social—ice-skating parties, roller-skating parties, outings, and dances like the one shown here to celebrate a change in leadership. From left to right are Anne Marie Aubin, Ray LaBelle, Mary Lou Bush, and Matt Smith, who ultimately progressed from youth council president to Speaker of the Rhode Island House of Representatives. (Courtesy of St. Michael's Church.)

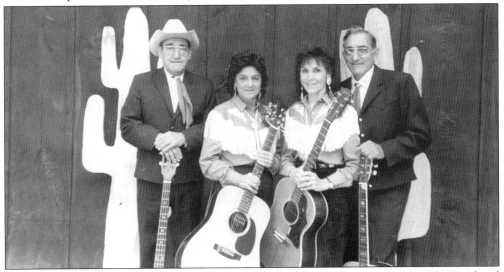

By the mid-1950s, rock and roll was the rage in South Providence, but this densely populated urban neighborhood produced a regionally popular country and western group at the same time. The Zacks—short for Zacharian—lived on Potters Avenue at the corner of Broad Street over the family market, which Peter Zacharian had originally operated at 975 Eddy Street. Eddie Zacharian (left) and his brother Richie "Cousin Richie" returned from navy service in World War II and teamed with their sisters Maril (left) and Babs to form the Hayloft Jamboree. In their heyday, the Zacks enjoyed a coast-to-coast radio audience on NBC and were frequently seen on WJAR-TV. Over the years, they have recorded for Columbia, Decca, and MCA Records. (Courtesy of Edward Lorello.)

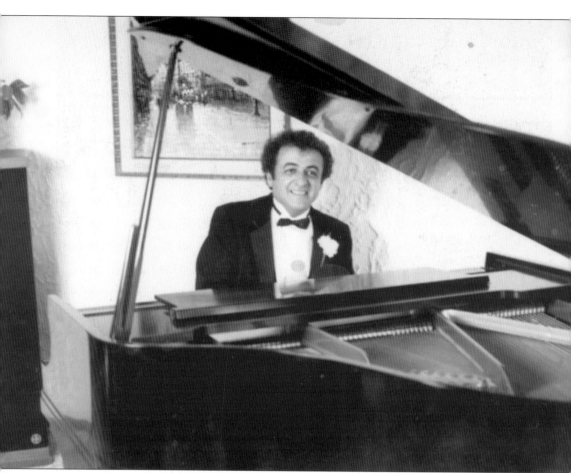

Stan Gurnick, who lived at 40 Reynolds Avenue, was a well-known local pianist. Completely self-taught, Gurnick performed at many area venues including the Club El Rio at Trinity Square and the Celebrity Club. In addition to playing for Gordon MacRae and Ginger Rogers at the Warwick Musical Theater, Gurnick appeared with many stars in the New England area, most notably Johnny Cash and Patsy Cline (in Boston), Connie Francis (in Providence), Jackie Wilson (in Fall River), and Bobby Darin and Fabian (at Rocky Point Park in Warwick). Gurnick put aside a musical career for one in finance, eventually earning a doctorate in business education at Indiana University in 1974. He coauthored several CPA study texts and a highly regarded book on franchising with Bob Dias from Briggs Street, a CPA who became the chief accountant for the Lawrence Welk enterprises and a writer of country songs. Gurnick taught at one of the City Colleges of Chicago for nearly three decades and became an expert in federal income taxation. The "Tax Doc" and several of his wealthy Chicago-area clients, most notably Benedict Gambino and John Finnegan, invested heavily in the revitalization of South Providence from 1990 onward. (Courtesy of Dr. Stan Gurnick.)

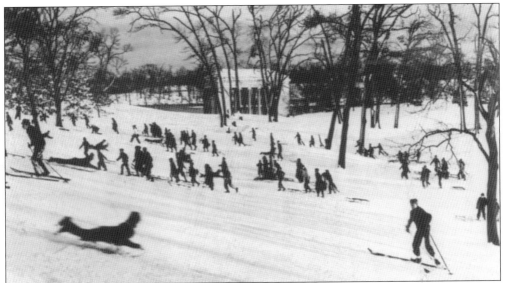

A favorite winter pastime for neighborhood children was sledding at nearby Roger Williams Park. Although just beyond the borders of South Providence, the park was an easy trek south on Prairie Avenue to Broad Street and the entrance to nearly 450 acres of hills for sledding and lakes for skating and ice fishing—not to mention the small zoo and the merry-go-round that the park contained. The most beautiful setting in the park was the amphitheater of the Temple to Music, where these youngsters make the most of a cold winter's day. (Courtesy of the Roger Williams Park Museum.)

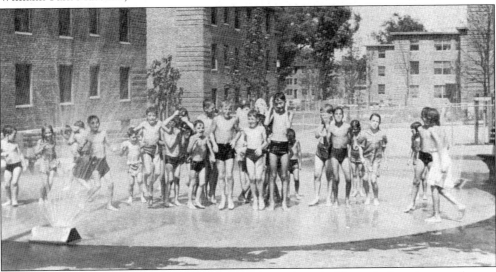

During the summer, the children of South Providence got relief from the heat in several ways: they took to the large pool at South Providence Recreation Center on Dudley Street or the much smaller version in Richardson Park; they braved the toxic and polluted water of the Providence River and jumped off the Allens Avenue docks; they turned on the fire hydrants; or they stood (as here) in the several showers located in the Roger Williams Housing Project. At mid-century, trips to ocean beaches were rare, but the Richardson Park baseball team usually got one day at Scarborough and a lunch at the Junior Police Camp for winning the recreation department's Playground League Championship. (Courtesy of the Providence Housing Authority.)

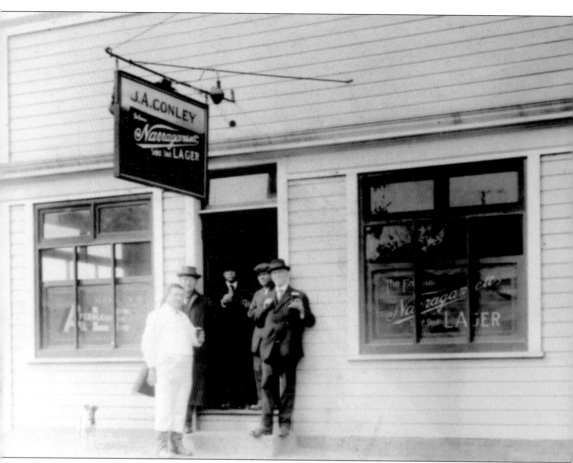

John Augustus "Jack" Conley operated this bar on Kay Street at the foot of Thurbers Avenue from 1915 until 1924. He was born at 37 Clinton Street (now Willard Avenue) in Dogtown on May 16, 1875, and moved to Burgess Cove as a young man. Jack was a locally famous wrestler and may have inspired his cousin George to embark upon the same career path. When Prohibition came in 1919, Conley's Bar and others like it—throughout the neighborhood and around the country—were doomed. Jack served soft drinks until 1924, and no drinks thereafter. (Courtesy of Julia Maney Conley.)

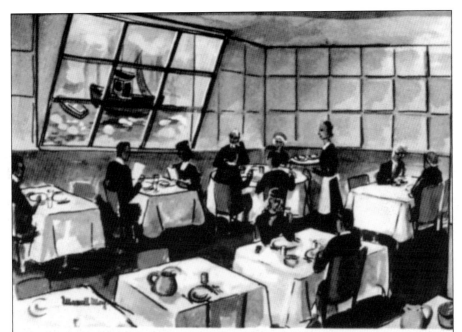

PAINTING BY MAXWELL MAYS

Johnson's Hummocks Grill ONE of the largest year-round seafood restaurants in New England, this establishment requires eight dining rooms to accommodate its patrons. One of the unusual dishes is a miniature clambake. Henry Johnson is the owner and manager.

Lunch, dinner daily until 1:00 a.m.

BAKED OYSTERS ON HALF SHELL

32 fresh oysters on the half shell
¼ pound each, butter, lard
1 or 2 cloves garlic, finely chopped
2 tablespoons parsley, chopped
1 tablespoon Worcestershire sauce
½ teaspoon each, salt and paprika
1 ounce anisette
1 ounce gin

¼ pound cracker meal
    Dash of Tabasco (optional)
Cream butter and lard; add remaining ingredients (except oysters) and mix well. Drop teaspoon of dressing on each oyster. Bake at 400° until dressing turns golden brown (8 or 10 minutes). Garnish with lemon wedge. Serves 4.

1 **NORTHEAST**   *245 Allens Avenue, Providence, Rhode Island*
36

Johnson's Hummocks Restaurant, founded in 1905 by Henry Johnson at 245 Allens Avenue (U.S. Route 1A), was by far South Providence's largest and most famous eatery. In fact, it boasted a national reputation, as indicated by this 1954 entry, painted by Maxwell Mays, in the Ford Motor Company's *Treasury of Favorite Recipes from Famous Eating Places*. As business waned in the 1960s, Johnson's inaugurated a dinner theater directed by Betsy Argo. Despite this innovation, the restaurant did not survive the decade. Today the building is occupied by a strip club called Cheaters. (Courtesy of Gail C. Conley.)

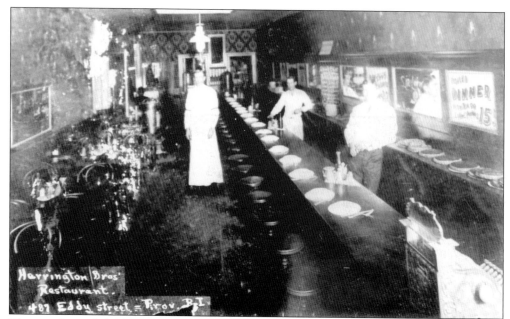

The members of the Harrington clan were Providence's leading Irish-American restaurateurs. Nine of the 10 sons of Patrick Harrington were full or part owners of Providence restaurants. In this 1905 photograph, from left to right, Pat, James, and Tom await customers in their Harrington Brothers Restaurant located at 487 Eddy Street, a site later occupied by Ward's Baking Company, makers of Tip-Top Bread. The menu on the chalkboard suggests some Irish influence—lamb pie and a 15¢ plate of ham and cabbage. (Courtesy of Mr. and Mrs. Thomas A. Harrington.)

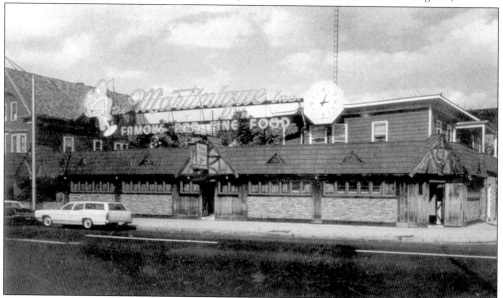

This postcard view shows the Martinique Restaurant at the corner of Broad Street and Massie Avenue during the 1950s, the peak of its prosperity. With Johnson's Hummocks, it was one of the two upscale neighborhood restaurants. In addition, it served as a meeting place and a watering hole for local politicians. The business survived until 1979, and eventually the building was demolished. Residential housing now occupies the site. (Courtesy of the authors.)

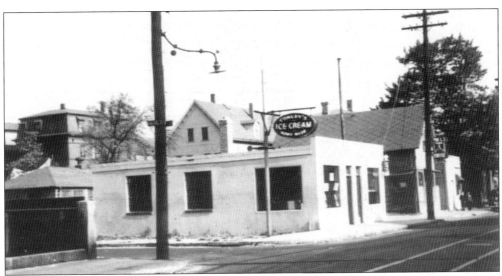

Lower South Providence had two major ice-cream parlors where the youth of the neighborhood could rendezvous and hang out. One cool spot was Conley's Ice Cream Parlor, opened in 1947 by Thomas and Julia Conley at 165 Thurbers Avenue. Their first soda jerk was famous baseball executive Lou Gorman. He was replaced by the Conleys' nephew Patrick. The store catered mainly to the residents of the Roger Williams Housing Project, so when the tenancy in that facility declined drastically, so did business. Conley's closed in 1965, less than two decades after its promising start. In 1969, the building was demolished along with Mills Coffee and Ben Jackvony's Wonder Bar to make way for a Mobil gas station that was itself replaced by a Burger King. (Courtesy of Julia Maney Conley.)

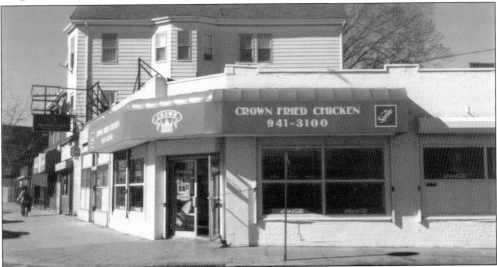

Cole's Ice Cream Parlor at the corner of Broad and Gallup Streets, where owner Tom Fogarty and manager Bob Carroll dispensed banana splits, coffee cabinets, and good will, was even livelier than Conley's for two good reasons: Broad Street was busier than Thurbers Avenue, and while Conley's was a gathering place for males of all ages, more young ladies frequented Cole's. Notwithstanding its popularity and the draw provided by Bessie's Variety Store next door, Cole's also folded, but the building survived. Today Crown Fried Chicken occupies the space. (Courtesy of the authors.)

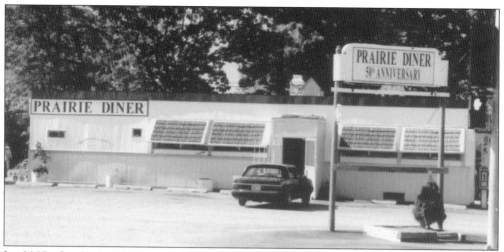

In 2005, the Prairie Diner on the southwest corner of Public Street celebrated its 50th anniversary. In 2006, it closed to make way for a much-needed redevelopment project designed to bring health-related businesses to this major neighborhood crossroads. At mid-century, busy Greenspan's Drug Store operated on the northeast corner of this intersection, and popular Webb's Cafe was located directly across Prairie Avenue from the diner. Webb's former site has long been a heavily littered vacant lot. Another noted diner, just beyond the borders of South Providence, was operated by Harry E. Burns. The now demolished Burns Pullman Diner, at 1209 Broad Street near the entrance to Roger Williams Park, was a favorite late-night eatery for patrons from Providence's entire Southside. (Courtesy of the authors.)

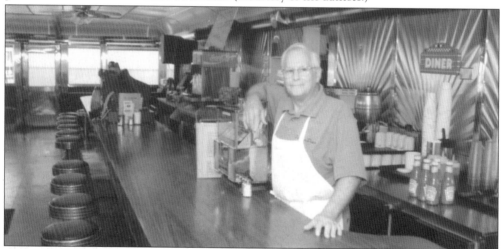

Dick Mahar opened the Seaplane Diner in 1935 on the easterly (or water) side of Allens Avenue. It derived its name from the aircraft that used to land and take off on the nearby Providence River. After the disastrous Hurricane of 1938, the diner was moved to its present location on the westerly side of Allens Avenue. John Avery acquired the business in 1973 and brought a larger diner to the site. Since 1975, the Seaplane has been operated by Bob Arena (shown here), who recently handed over the reins to his son, Mike, and Dave Penta. Of all the 1950s purveyors of food or drink in South Providence, the only survivors are the Seaplane and the Standard Liquor Store, established in 1937 at the corner of Eddy Street and Potters Avenue by the Rainone family. The oldest-surviving retail store of all is Check the Florist, which has operated its small shop at 342 Public Street since 1928. (Courtesy of the authors.)